ENDURANCE

An Autistic Autobiography

Lucien-Bracquemont

Contents

INTRODUCTION

At the suggestion of my counselor, who has a Licensed Clinical Social Worker's degree, I have decided to write an autobiography of my life as an autistic person. I am middle-aged, am on the autistic spectrum (Asperger's Syndrome), and though every attempt to enter the middle class has failed miserably, I have an IQ (intelligence quotient) of 132-136, and my forte, possibly my only forte, is an unusually strong command of the English language along with highly articulate writing and analytical abilities. In nearly everything else, I am below average at best.

There are many skeletons in my closet, especially from my early teenage years, and I seek neither fame nor extravagant fortune. I do not want to be treated differently for being autistic, either to be treated as less than others or to be celebrated as a hero. This work, however, will be an articulate voice for the disabled and the working class. Though I had tremendous social and developmental problems, no one suspected that I was autistic until I was 49, and I did not receive a diagnosis until I was 51.

The overwhelmingly large majority of personal names and place names have been changed to protect the innocent and the not-so-innocent.

CHAPTER ONE

The earliest recollections of my childhood are those on the lake in a small town in New England. I lived there until I was nearly four years of age. I cannot remember my father from that early, but have many memories of my mother and Mrs. Smith, who was our baby sitter, and my next-door neighbor, "Uncle" Lester.

Though I was very small, I remember grabbing a bag of fertilizer from Uncle Lester, but he quickly ran after me and grabbed it from me. During my time at this home Uncle Lester had installed two large cement figures resembling lions at our entrance. They frightened me. I also remember once when my mother was cooking bacon. She poured the fat into a small can, which overflowed causing her to burn her hands. I thought that our babysitter Mrs. Smith was a witch. I collected milk cartons and small figures of cows.

My brother Sam was born when I was two and one-half years old, but I have few memories of him until we moved to another residence.

My parents told me that I did not start talking verbally until I was nearly three years old. I would learn many years later that this was a sign of autism.

We moved to our new residence in Cardiff, a nearby small city, in autumn of 1961. My father was a professional athlete. It has even been suggested that he may have been the basis for a minor character in a novel by Stephen King. (I do not recall which one.) He was therefore a local celebrity, and most people thought that he and we were at least twice as rich as we were. I was a highly unruly child, and was placed on Ritalin for many years. I was especially mean to my brother Sam. When I was five and Sam was three, I dropped a golf club on him when we were walking up a flight of stairs. I was far from being an angel, and gave both my parents and Sam a tremendous amount of grief.

I started Kindergarten at age five (5). I proved to be a well-above student academically in the next few years, which undoubtedly placated much of the wrath that some teachers would have had toward me. But I was often unruly. For a few days I often spun around, which the teachers disliked, and I was often hyper-active. I destroyed many books at home in my early childhood, but not at school.

I had significant problems with speech, and was in speech therapy for at least three years. Though my therapist, Mrs. O'Rourke, was extremely patient with me and very helpful, I resented being in speech therapy because it defined me as different and pulled me out of my regular classes. I had much difficulty with the "l" (as in light) and "r" (as in right) sounds as well as the "voiceless" "th" sound (as in think), but no problem with the "voiced th" as in "they." I addition, I could not, and cannot, whistle, but this was not an issue. I would learn decades later that my speech impediments were likely related to autism.

My strongest subject was spelling, and I consistently ranked at near the top in this subject.

The biggest domestic issue for me was my highly abusive behavior toward my brother Sam, and I often treated him very despicably. When he was approximately eight (8) I threw out of my second-story window his most cherished possession, his "Long John" hard plastic fire engine. It broke beyond repair into two pieces. And earlier I talked him into jumping out his bedroom on the second floor. My motive was not to do him bodily harm, but to use him as a "guinea pig" to see if rolling along the outside of the house was a safe way to exit from the second floor to the outside. Sam had to go to the emergency room at the local hospital.

My maternal grandmother, whom we called "Nunna," was very close to me, never slapped me, was highly affectionate to me, and I loved her dearly. She owned an apartment house which she received as a settlement from her divorce, and she had a tenant whom she had once considered marrying. "Jefferson" and she remained close friends, though, and since she did not have a car, Jeff very generously provided much transportation for her. Jeff also took my brother and me out shopping on Saturday morning for several months. Jeff often said to me, "I want you to stop abusing Sam." Once during my childhood, my mother told me that Nunna would probably die before I graduated from high school. This made me very sad.

When I was five years old, my mother became pregnant for a third time, though I was unaware of it. About this time, when my mother needed to get somewhere in a hurry, I threw her car keys into a snowbank. It took her a while to find the keys. Two or three years later, she reminded me of this incident but I had confused it with the time when she needed to get to the hospital quickly but had a miscarriage. For a few years, I thought that my mother had a miscarriage because she could not get to the hospital in time because I threw the keys into the snow; she later clarified that the two incidents were unrelated.

That year for Thanksgiving, my father and I went to visit his parents in Connecticut. At that time, one of my few enjoyments was playing with cellophane tape, especially if it was colored. I saw my mother place a roll of colored tape into a small pail. I thought that she was trying to take it from me, so I removed it when she was not looking. When we arrived in Connecticut, my father handed me the pail, and I learned why my mother had placed the roll of colored tape into the pail. I was highly disappointed that it was not there.

It had become obvious by the time I was ten (10) that my parents had deep marital issues and problems, and it was likely that my emotional, social, and developmental problems contributed to them. We were not a happy, "functional" family. I suspected that my parents would eventually become divorced.

On some episode of a television show, the name of which I cannot remember, there was a little boy who had a tape recorder. He recorded many conversations with his recorder hidden, and stunned people with his knowledge of these conversations. This continued for several days, and no adults suspected the boy's true method. This ended, however, when the boy hid his recorder under his parents' couch. They discussed their plans to divorce. The boy was heart-broken when he played the recording, and admitted to his parents his hidden recorder. I knew that it was only a matter of time before my parents divorced.

At school my least favorite classes were recess (if you can call it a class) and gymnasium. No one wanted to play with me at recess, and I performed very poorly at gym class, due to my well-below-average co-ordination. Whenever we played kickball,

all the students on the opposing team would move much closer to me, knowing that I could kick the ball neither far nor well.

Whenever recess was canceled due to inclement weather, the students would play board games inside, but no one ever wanted to play them with me. Whenever I see a "Candy Land" board set, it usually reminds me of this memory from my childhood. No one ever invited me to a birthday party, either.

Most of my teachers had mixed feelings toward me, finding me both highly disruptive but academically gifted. One teacher who obviously did not like me much was my fifth-grade teacher. Even though I was nearly a straight-A student, she placed me in the section for C-level students. She denounced my poor athletic ability when the class played baseball. However, much to my surprise, she once told me that a visiting teacher spoke of my as "the sweetest child that she ever knew." This was both puzzling and disturbing. For one thing, boys were not supposed to be "sweet." And if I was so "sweet," then how come my teacher did not like me and was so mean to me, and so were most of the students?

During the summers, my parents sent me to a day-time camp. I enjoyed this much better than I enjoyed school. Though I was never good at swimming, I enjoyed swimming and being in the water immensely. My least favorite event was baseball, at which I was extremely poor. After a while, I skipped it. Despite my poor co-ordination, though, I was passable in archery. I performed well with a bow and arrow, though not when I attempted to use a BB gun. We had crafts, at which I did at least average. At our camp we pretended to be Indians. We were divided by age into "tribes," and we wore feathered headdresses. One summer I became fascinated with Indians, and loved pretending to be an Indian. My near relatives and ancestors were of Irish, English, and French-Canadian ancestry, and informed me that we had no Indian ancestry. I would learn many years later, though, that my maternal grandmother Nunna, who was chiefly of English colonial ancestry, very likely had some Native American (Indian) ancestry. More on that to come later. I had happy times at camp, and when I was nine (9) years old I won a trophy for being the "Most Improved Camper."

[Update in 2023: I now realize that Native Americans and their white allies now regard such practices as "offensive cultural appropriation." No offense is intended to Native Americans; I was merely reflecting values of the 1960's. Indeed, my experiences at camp made me more aware of Native Americans.]

A few months earlier, when I was sick for several days, my grandmother thought that numismatics (coin collecting) might be an interesting hobby for me, and bought me an 1890 Indian Head cent and a couple other old coins. I quickly and deeply dived into numismatics. At summer camp, another camper who collected coins suggested that I meet him on Saturday at the local coin shop. I felt certain that mom would drive me there, but she refused to do so. On Monday, the camper asked why I did not meet him at the coin shop. This made me very sad. This keen interest in numismatics many years later turned out to be a mixed blessing at best. Far more to come on this subject.

Because I was a very picky eater, I did not eat with my family very often, unless we went out to eat. One of the rare occasions when I would eat with them was on Thanksgiving. On one Thanksgiving, while my father was washing the dishes, he accidentally placed a butter knife into the garbage disposer while it was turned on, which put ruined the edges of the knife. He made my mother use that knife on future occasions, even though my father was the one who ruined it.

For a short period of time, my parents forced me to eat supper with them and Sam, and to try new foods. One night, my father antagonized me by placing a frozen box in my face and saying, "Tomorrow night: Bavarian style beans and spaetzle." He did not carry through, though many years later I did try Bavarian style green beans and spaetzle and very much enjoyed them!

During this period in my life my parents took me for testing at a center approximately 60 miles from our home for possible brain deformities. The workers applied some strange glue to my hair to attach wires. The results were inconclusive.

My parents once bought me a chemistry set for Christmas. I was quite excited about it, but much to my disappointment, neither parent would ever help me use it.

My mother often criticized me, and rightly so, for my physical abuse of Sam. She even once said that she thought that I might have killed him if I could have done so.

Sometime shortly later my father stopped at our local movie theater to buy some tickets. While he was inside, my brother and I fought in the backseat of the car, and I was lying on my back, forcing my brother to the roof of the car with my legs. This upset my parents greatly.

An unfortunate incident took place outside of the local "Great A&P Tea Co." store, where some bullies beat me up. I was very often the victim of bullies, though I was a bully to my brother.

At the approximate age of ten, I saw a movie on a local station about Hitler and the Holocaust. This, of course, included Hitler's extreme hatred of Jewish people, and his extermination of millions of them. The movie included a scene of Nazis' throwing bricks through a synagogue window, followed by a frightening scene where Nazis entered a Jewish home and grabbed and carried out a highly frightened older woman. It is frightening indeed how some people become filled with hatred toward others and dehumanize them. I now consider this scene more frightening than I did at the time.

During this time I became highly frightened of the dark and of the night. For a few weeks, I even tucked in the sheets of my bed so that they covered all of my body, including even my head.

It was about this time that the "Women's Lib" movement was starting to take on steam, and my mother drank very, very deeply of it. This created immense conflict between my parents, and between my mother and me. Had I been several years older it would have troubled me far less, but being a pre-teen I greatly resented the rhetoric of women's libbers who regarded raising children as an "obstacle to fulfillment," who regarded marriage, family, and children as a "male chauvinist fraud" to keep women away from "highly fulfilling careers." I realize that since 1984 it has been the ultimate heresy to those who are "politically correct" to regard feminism as anything less than absolutely sacrosanct and immune to criticism, but I include this because of its autobiographical significance. At any rate, the extreme emphasis that women's libbers placed on "self-fulfillment" seemed very much to mean that children and their welfare were unimportant to feminists at the time, and many of them at the time were openly anti-family and anti-marriage, which earned them much criticism even from the news media, but the feminists learned to become far more subtle in later years. Feminists seemed to dislike childbearing; it was common at the time for them to say, "I'm not a baby machine."

Because of my poor co-ordination and because I was certain to be ridiculed because of my poor performance, I rarely developed any interest in sports, even though males are "supposed" to be highly interested in sports. Not only did this affect my self-esteem, but also my sociability.

I continued to visit my grandmother and Jeff on the weekends, and Jeff would often take us on road trips. One occasion that I can recall is when we were traveling approximately 35 miles from home. Jeff pointed to a house where someone that he previously knew was living. Jeff said, "I used to know the man who lives there. He had a promising career as an electrician ahead of him. Unfortunately, he drank it all away."

During the summer between fifth and sixth grades, my brother very kindly taught me how to ride a bicycle. Even though he was younger that I, he mastered it far earlier, and we all knew that for some reason (namely, poor co-ordination), I was incapable of riding a bicycle at an earlier age. I quickly enjoyed my new skill immeasurably.

Late in the sixth grade, several students began to tease me unmercifully about how I loved and wanted to marry Cheryl, a girl who sat directly behind me in class. Cheryl was a very fine girl, and she ignored those who teased her, but I was very angry about the teasing, and everyone knew it, and it made school very difficult for me. The antagonism was so intense that school officials let me leave early from school each day and to arrive a few minutes late to avoid antagonism from other students. However, as children turn into teenagers, their attitude toward peers of the opposite sex changes radically. Had this happened two or three years later, it would not have bothered me much at all.

On one occasion, my parents went with some of their friends to a fancy restaurant approximately 45 miles away. The next day, I heard my mother complain to my father about how he humiliated and ridiculed her in the presence of many people at the restaurant. I also heard her complain about it to several people on the telephone. I clearly and confidently sided with my mother. In the late afternoon, I spoke to Nunna on the telephone and told her about the unfortunate incident, clearly sympathizing with my mother. Mom overheard me, and slapped me on the face. I felt that this was highly unfair on her part, since I sided with her. Both my parents slapped both my brother and me several hundred times on the face and elsewhere in our pre-teen years, usually with their hands but occasionally with a belt. This must be understood in the context of the times, when corporal punishment by parents was culturally acceptable. Once my father even pressed an English muffin against my face, because I did not eat a sufficient breakfast that morning.

A local television station broadcast reruns of *Gilligan's Island,* which shortly became my favorite television show of all times. Earlier my mother and I often watched it during its airing on CBS nationally during its second and third seasons (1965-67.) I had never seen a first season episode until December of 1969, and though the words of the beginning and ending theme songs were similar, the music was very different. It was hard to get out of my head once it got there. I quickly developed a strong preference for the second and third seasons, since I liked their music and theme songs much better. On my thirteenth birthday, our local affiliate broadcast the episode "The Producer," a third-season episode, and this was the first "new" (second or third season episode) after the station had aired dozens of "old" (first season episodes). I loved this episode, and have always cherished it as a special, wonderful birthday memory.

In the sixth grade my once-excellent grades began to decline, and I became a mediocre student. This was probably due to intense conflict with other students, who were highly unfriendly and verbally and physically abusive to me. One kid even forced my head onto the sidewalk pavement several times, saying "We aren't on school grounds now!"

A local recently opened supermarket had an automatic front door. While my mother was shopping inside, I enjoyed jumping onto the mat which caused the door to open, then jumping off it so that it would immediately close. This happened at least a dozen times. Surprisingly, no one told me to stop doing it.

CHAPTER TWO
Just Before The Rupture

As I entered grade seven at the junior high school (now called "middle school" in most communities,) my grades continued to decline, and my conflicts with other students accelerated. The seventh grade was divided into many sections with regard to perceived academic ability. Mine was "71-B," the second highest division. There were approximately 30 children in my division, and we attended most of the same classes, except those boys and girls attended different gymnasium classes, and during the second semester the boys studied wood shop while the girls attended home economics.

Once during wood shop while the teacher was out of the room for a few minutes, one student and I became involved in a vicious physical fight. This quickly stopped after the instructor returned. He said to me, "Get over there, you pill!" (I actually found this somewhat amusing, and he later signed my yearbook, at my request, "To my favorite 'pill.'")

A very kind man who worked for the local Parks and Recreation department would pick me up for a couple hours each Monday during the summer and take me with him as he did chores at local public parks. He was engaged to a French-Canadian woman, Lorraine Thibodeau, who was also very kind and generous to me. Once Lorraine treated me to lunch at a local A&W take-out, and took me to a local private beach opened to the public. This was one of the most special occurrences of my childhood.

My parents' marital problems progressively got worse. In October, 1971, I saw my father packing his luggage to go somewhere. My mother promptly told Sam and me that they were separating, and she was not sure where my Dad would go. Sam and I were both devastated, and begged Mom to let Dad return home. The next day was a school holiday, but Sam and I were both very unhappy. We begged our mother to allow my father to return home. We learned that Dad had spent the night at a motel in a nearby town. Fortunately, after seeing her children's unhappiness, Mom relented and allowed Dad to return home. Sam and I were both relieved. Many years later I praised my mother for allowing this, stating that the subsequent lives of both Sam and me would have been far worse, and to express my appreciation many years later I gave my mother a silver medallion specially engraved with this date.

During this year my father took me to shop for clothes, and I made the disastrous and unfortunate choice to buy a pink shirt. I wore it to school only once, and one student frightened me by his comments about it. For that reason, I never wore that shirt again until after the "rupture" started. Looking back, I realize that he did me very much of a favor, and deeply regret that I later rejected his advice.

This was many years before VCR's (video cassette recorders) became available, so I did the most that was technologically possible at the time and made audio recordings of *Gilligan's Island* and *F Troop* which were my favorite television shows of that time. When these shows were not being aired, listening to their audio recordings was my favorite solitary pastime. Before much longer, they would become one of the few sources of enjoyment in my life.

Because the summer camp which I attended for the previous five years did not cater to children over the age of twelve, I did not attend any camp this summer.

Then came autumn, and I entered the eighth grade. This time I was placed in the highest division of students, but I became increasingly disruptive, ill-behaved and indifferent to studying and learning. Our English teacher, Mrs. Chase, was very young and very beautiful in appearance. However, though we students preferred younger and more physically attractive teachers, we had more respect for the older teachers. At the coaxing of other students, on two occasions I placed a thumbtack on Mrs. Chase's chair and even insulted her in front of the class, but she never punished me. Since I admired her physical beauty, I even told her once during class, "You're cute!" I was very popular in English class when we had spelling bees, as I was nearly always the best student at spelling. We would divide into teams, and I would be the first to be selected, and was called the team's "mascot." Other than this, I had become a very poor student both academically and socially.

Though I do not remember this incident, my mother claimed many times that I pushed a girl down a staircase who had antagonized me.

I was so disruptive, and the other students so antagonistic to me, that my homeroom teacher allowed me to eat lunch alone in our homeroom, even though he was away for the lunch period.

I did fairly well in our introductory French class, and during February of this year my Father and I traveled to southern France and Monaco for one week. We arrived in Nice on the French Riviera, traveled to Marseille to the west and to Monaco to the east. On the way from Marseille to Nice we drove through a town named Cannes. I had learned from an episode of *Gilligan's Island* that Cannes was the site of an international film festival. I had never seen the name *Cannes* in print, but immediately recognized the name when I saw it at the Cannes town line. Later we drove to Monaco. The region between Nice and Monaco was very mountainous, and richly beautiful. There were three routes between Nice and Monaco, the *haute corniche,* the *mid corniche,* and the *basse corniche.* We took the *haute (high) corniche* to Monaco, and will never forget the breathtaking scenery. Since I was the passenger and Dad had to pay attention to the road, I am sure that I enjoyed it far more than he did. We returned to Nice on the *basse (low) corniche.*

When I returned home, I was suddenly very popular for a few days in my French class. I brought back many photographs from France which I shared with my classmates, and the teacher used an overhead projector to show them to the class. I thoroughly enjoyed France, and felt sure that this would be the happiest year of my life. Instead, several weeks later I would receive the most devastating news ever.

Shortly afterward, my grandmother Nunna sold her large apartment house and moved to a much smaller house on the street next to ours. This made it possible to visit her far more often. She no longer had Jeff as a tenant, and she and Jeff had become increasingly alienated from each other.

My parents renovated the basement of our home, and my brother moved into a beautiful new room in the basement, which he very much enjoyed.

It was well heated. Previously he lived in a much smaller room on the second floor next to my bedroom.

Meanwhile, conditions were deteriorating at a frightening pace. In late April I wanted to watch a certain television show in my parent's bedroom. (They were away for a few hours.) This station was available only on cable television. My brother wanted to watch a different show, on a local station. He could easily have watched it in his own room on his own television set, but insisted on using the TV in my parents' room. We started arguing and fighting violently, until I threw a butcher's knife at Sam from across the room. I knew that I would shortly be in deep trouble with my parents. The trouble would turn out to be far worse than I could have expected. My brother had to go to the hospital though there was no permanent damage except for a scratch that took many years to disappear.

On a Saturday morning in May I was watching an episode of the cartoon *Archie.* On this episode, Archie's friend Jughead was expelled from school. Shortly he was shivering in extreme fear at having to notify his parents. This would, in only a few hours, hauntingly resonate with me.

That Saturday evening, my parents had a private conference with me in their bedroom. They gave me that most frightful, devastating news ever. They were planning to send me to an institution for badly troubled and ill-behaving children far away. It was not yet sure when I would be admitted, but next Wednesday they would take me there for tests. Wednesday came and went. I saw the home, Genevaville, in Baggerston. It did not seem quite so frightening, but appearances were deceiving. The faculty there assured my parents and me that they would give us a two-week notice before admitting me. I took their word for it, much to my disappointment and sense of false security. They gave us only a four-day notice.

I finished the eighth grade, though I had grades that were mostly "D" or "F." The tests given to me at Genevaville, though, indicated that I was ready for ninth grade. Had my parents not planned to send me to Genevaville I probably would have needed to repeat eighth grade, if I had been lucky enough to be allowed to do so! Two years later my mother told me that the junior high school was planning to expel me. Because of the plans to send me to Genevaville, no such procedures were necessary.

In the meantime, I had a carefree life for a few weeks, blissful (and blissfully unaware) that the worst experiences of my life would be just around the corner.

CHAPTER THREE
The Rupture

The night before I was admitted to Genevaville, I slept better than nearly any night ever. This is indeed perplexing.

We arrived at Genevaville at 2:00 p.m. We shortly met the cottage parents, the Van Pelters, in the building where I would be staying. When learning how restrictive life would be at Genevaville, I became very angry and threw a small metal chest on the floor. Mr. Van Pelter became tremendously angry at me. I instantly cried, and cried for much of the next two hours.

I met with Mr. MacGregor, a staff member who told me much about Genevaville, and told me that I would likely spend one to two years there.

Only two days later, most of the students and faculty at Genevaville traveled by bus to a lake approximately 30 miles away. I went separately and later because the campus nurse wanted to see me for an exam. This was requested by Mrs. Van Pelter, who felt that I had discolored skin due to lack of nutrition. In fact, I was an extremely picky and under-nourished child. I would learn many years later that this was due to autism, as autistic people have a strong resistance to foods with textures that they find disagreeable; they are highly sensitive to "textures." I rode in a "mini-bus" with a faculty member. I had a wonderful time at the beach, and rode back on the bus.

The next day, Thursday, disaster struck. An ill-behaved bully found me an easy prey due to my small under-nourished size and dragged me on the ground by my knees with no provocation on my part.

I rejected the not-so-friendly but highly valuable feedback from the student in the seventh grade and started wearing the pink shirt. One of my roommates told me several times that he hated that shirt on me, but I stubbornly and defiantly continued to wear it for at least two or three weeks. It was not long before half the students started severely persecuting me for being gay, which unfortunately persisted for many months. There were dozens of highly despicable, incorrigibly unkind students at Genevaville, and their extremely low character was frightening indeed. This could not help but cause me to have a highly cynical outlook on humanity, which took decades to overcome. And, for the most part, the girls were equally as base and despicable as the boys. It was very frightening to realize just how cruel and hateful people can be.

For better or worse, the faculty were of the prevailing philosophy of the times. They largely held the simplistic view that if victims would merely "ignore" the bullies, then the bullies would stop antagonizing the victims. Rarely were the bullies or antagonists ever punished or even disciplined. The tendency was to blame the victims.

I did make several friends quickly after arriving at Genevaville, but most of them quickly turned against me; they were two-faced. Mrs. Van Pelter told me that I was the "sickest child" that she ever knew. I quickly developed an interest in playing cards, especially gin rummy and rummy 500.

There were very few, compassionate children at Genevaville. One of the few kind children was Vicki. I was not that nice to her at first but she persisted in being nice to be and became a faithful friend. We kept in touch for a year or so after she left Genevaville. Vicki was one of the finest people that I ever knew.

I was quickly assigned a case worker, Dr. Dubois. I met with him the second Monday at Genevaville. He gave me much encouragement, and I responded very enthusiastically, but with way too much optimism.

Shortly after I arrived, the singing group Chicago released a song, "Saturday in the Park." The "Fourth of July" was a prominent theme in this song. For that reason, this song made me immensely sad, as it reminded me of how much happier I was on July 4, before I was sent to Genevaville.

Several weeks later, school began. I entered the ninth grade (freshman year) at Baggerston Academy. The students at Baggerston Academy were far more normal than those at Genevaville, but they had their share of antagonistic bullies. There were a few that, with no provocation, antagonized me and made life frightful and miserable. The Genevaville bus made our arrival at school each day far more conspicuous that would have been necessary. Students at Baggerston Academy knew that we Genevaville students were "different" and we had a bad reputation. One day while several of us were on the bus, we heard a student shout to another student, not a Genevaville student, "You're getting on the wrong bus. That's not the Genevaville bus." This offended several of us.

One faculty member who took an interest in me and was highly kind to me was Mr. Devereux. (Not his real name, though his real name was an English name of Norman origin.) He was assigned to me as my guidance counselor, and gave me much encouragement.

A few months later, Dr. Dubois and two other faculty members, Mr. Thompson and Miss Lindsay, formed a group of about eight teenaged students, including me. I enjoyed this group very much. I also got to know many students, both within and without the group, much better. Vicki was a member of this group, and I learned that Vicki lost her father to disease very young, and then lost her step-father not much later. Vicki was possibly unique among the students at Genevaville for her kindness and compassion. Mrs. Van Pelter once met with me privately and told me that every student in our cottage had given much grief to his or her parents. I shortly learned that the large majority of Genevaville students were from broken homes or from widowed parents; I was indeed among very much of a minority by coming from an intact home with two biological parents. Most of the students, nearly all of them, had faced intense learning problems and/or emotional abuse. Most of them had become incorrigibly hardened and anti-social and intensely cruel. Vicki was an exception. Her intense emotional issues had caused her to become patient and compassionate toward others, rather than mean toward them. She did, however, have a learning disability, and stayed back in school for two years. She hoped to become a nurse, and worked for a few hours as a candy striper at a local hospital on the weekends.

Mrs. Van Pelter once confided to me about a girl in my cottage. The girl had been told that her parents had died in the fire. Mrs. Van Pelter told me that in truth her parents did not die, but fled to another state. The authorities never caught up with the parents, and the parents abandoned their children to die, but I must keep this secret and never tell this girl the truth. Ugly truths like this increased in me even deeper feelings of cynicism.

I must admit that I engaged in some highly asinine behavior. One Sunday at lunch, a part-time cottage parent complained about an unruly girl who caused trouble while he was driving students to church. He said, "[Darn] that Gertrude…She threw a bean or something at the back of my head. I stopped the bus and she fell on the floor, getting her dress wet and messy." I thought that this was hilarious! For the next several days, I would tap people on the back of the head and say "bean!"

My academic performance at Baggerston Academy was average; not outstanding or poor; but nothing exciting. I never made the honor roll. My least favorite class was, not surprisingly, gymnasium. I had to attend it four times weekly. I was the victim of some but not intense ridicule, and was always the last to be chosen for any team.

I learned to eat more foods and overcame my fear of trying new foods. I ate hamburgers, chicken, popcorn, rice, and even pizza for the first time. Had it not been for Genevaville, I likely would have died young from malnutrition.

A very generous owner of a pizzeria in a neighboring town had a fine tradition of inviting all the students and faculty from Genevaville for a night of free pizza each December near Christmas. He closed his pizzeria to the general public on Monday night of this week to reserve it for us. This was the first time that I ever ate pizza.

Even though dozens of students at both Genevaville and Baggerston Academy falsely thought that I was gay, Mrs. Van Pelter knew better. She encouraged me to find a girlfriend many times, especially toward the end of my stay at Genevaville. She did, however, imply at times that I did not fulfill the stereotypes to which boys should supposedly conform.

Over the next several months I made steady progress in many ways.

For the freshman year, I earned a grade point average of about 2.54; intense mediocrity, but passable.

During finals week at Baggerston Academy, on a particular day the the Van Pelters wanted me to come back to Genevaville for lunch, and then return to high school for the other final. I, however, decided to stay at school because I was afraid that I would encounter some enemies if I returned to the Genevaville campus for lunch. When I arrived in the late afternoon, Mr. Van Pelter was highly angry at me. He informed me that when I go home to Cardiff for the next time, I would have to leave two-and-one-half hours later than usual for punishment, or if my father decided to pick me up, he would have to wait for two hours to see me do menial work before he could leave campus with me. To me, this was an agreeable trade-off, though I did not share this opinion with Mr. Van Pelter. His continued anger at this minor incident seemed unreasonable to me.

The authorities at Genevaville allowed us one weekend a month to go home, sometimes longer for school holidays and early summer. Sometimes I left on the bus, or arrived on the bus, or my parents picked me up or drove me back to Genevaville. Signs near Genevaville reminded me that I was returning to a highly painful and unpleasant place. One of these signs near campus was for a new car dealership. This dealership, though nearly 150 miles from Cardiff, widely advertises in many parts of the state, including Cardiff. Whenever I see one of its television ads, it always reminds me that its sign was an unwelcome reminder of my return to Genevaville.

My second summer at Genevaville arrived. Many of my worst archenemies has left by now, and most of the new arrivals knew not about the skeletons in my closet, and were far, far less antagonistic.

In September of this year, a truly wonderful and positive thing happened which immensely improved my life. A very sweet and lovable girl approximately my age, Danielle, arrived and we instantly became close friends. She was the daughter of a college professor. She was very thin and under-developed in appearance. I would learn years later that she had anorexia. One could tell from the intense sadness in her voice and her thin appearance that she suffered tremendous emotional depression, which would cause her to lose her appetite and thus much weight. For the first time, I felt immense compassion for another child. I really loved her.

The faculty at Genevaville, especially Mrs. Van Pelter, noticed immense changes in me after Danielle arrived. She praised me for being Danielle's friend, but stated that Danielle was a "very sick girl." On Friday night Danielle and I played cards, and up to that time I had never felt closer to any human being (except relatives). The other students had noticed how close she and I had become, and even pejoratively suggested that we were so stuck on each other that we ignored the other residents.

Sadly, Danielle's friendship proved too good to last. She ran away from Genevaville shortly after. She was absent for several days until her parents returned her to the campus. For the next week, she was forced to do boring, menial chores for several hours and was kept from socializing with other residents as punishment for running away.

A few days later, a student named Vincent arrived. He was two years older than I. We became friends quickly, but monopolized much of my social time. When Danielle was later free to socialize, Vincent kept me from associating with her.

Vincent could have gotten me into some trouble. He did not get along well with faculty and staff members, one of whom said to me, "I'm going to re-arrange his face shortly." Vincent used highly abusive language in describing staff members, and seemed highly prejudiced against anyone with gray hair. Sometimes he even insulted adults to their faces. For some reason, many staff members allowed him to get away with such. Maybe they thought that he was incorrigibly ignorant, or maybe they feared him.

Though Vincent was a low achiever academically, he tried very hard to study. He deserved credit for that. He usually studied at least one hour longer than cottage rules required. He was often the last student to go to bed. One night, Mr. Van Pelter said to his wife, "Tell Webster (Vincent) to go to bed." I thought it was inappropriate for Mr. Van Pelter to ridicule Vincent thus when Vincent was trying so hard to succeed.

During the first quarter of my sophomore year at Baggerston Academy I once again performed average academically. I usually did very well at

French, but for a period of about two weeks I performed very poorly, though this did not last long. I discussed this with my guidance counselor Mr. Devereux, who told me much to my surprise that he always found French to be a difficult subject. He said, "I never did very well at French." I had assumed all along that Mr. Devereux was from a French heritage; in addition he grew up in Lewiston, then a heavily French town in Maine. I replied, "With a name like Devereux and you performed poorly in French?" He responded, "What does that have to do with it?" I said, "You must be French," to which he responded, "No, I'm all English." I then said, "Devereux is a French name." "I never knew that it was." "Well, it looks French." He then said, "Maybe it is. But all my ancestors were English." This would turn out to be a history lesson; several months later I learned that Normans named d'Evereux invaded England in 1066, which explains why people named Devereux have an English heritage despite the French appearance of the name.

Shortly afterwards, with no notice and much to my disappointment, Danielle's parents chose to remove her from Genevaville, and she moved to another state to live with her grandmother. Her parents came during the school day to get her. She requested to say good-bye to me, but the authorities refused to co-operate. This was a big loss to Danielle and me alike.

No one among my peers ever became as close to me as Danielle. I had no precedent for predicting what this would lead to. I had a deep seated fear that we would become so close that we would eventually get married. For this reason, Danielle's departure provided some relief. However, looking back, I feel that Danielle was the best thing that had ever happened to me up to that time, and that I never would have amounted to much of anything were it not for her. I am deeply indebted to her for changing my life indefinitely.

While this first quarter of the school year (but my last quarter at Baggerston Academy) was generally marked by less harassment and hostility from other students, gym class was an exception. When filing from the locker room to the gym, students would often harass and ridicule me, so I waited a short period to file out. I would wait, then file out before the teacher could notice. But for about three days in a row, he noticed. He shouted, "Hey, Bracquemont, what's going on?" I told him why I waited, but he was not too sympathetic.

Disaster struck as I returned from a weekend home to Genevaville on Sunday for my last week there. About halfway between Cardiff and

Baggerston, a pedophile, probably in his 50's, got onto the bus and sat next to me. He placed a jacket over his and my mid-section and molested me several times. Due at least partly to the intense attitudes of the time of the culture in general, and at Genevaville in particular that children must be totally submissive to adults, I did nothing to resist him. I did not tell anyone on the bus, let alone shout. I was passive in letting him violate me. When I arrived back at Genevaville I told the cottage mother about it in vague terms, and when I arrived home next week for good, I told my mother about it. She responded that I should have told the authorities that I was being molested. Until then, I had never even heard the term "molest." Looking back on it, I realize that I did not dare to say anything while on the bus. Sometimes I regret that I let him get away with it, but on the other hand I was starting my final week at Genevaville and just wanted to get home as quickly as possible. I did not want to be dragged to a court setting nearly 150 miles from home. In those days, very few people would take the word of a minor against that of an adult. I regret that my passivity and quietness made it possible for him to victimize other children.

On Friday of that week, I was discharged from Genevaville, and returned to Cardiff. This was an extremely happy day for me.

I must admit that I did become far more sociable as a result of Genevaville, as well as learning to enjoy many more activities and improving my diet. And I doubt that I would have ever amounted to much if I had not been for my close friendship with Danielle. And I must admit that, for the most part, I was a truly vile person much of the time before I knew her. She radically transformed me.

CHAPTER FOUR
Back Home

My parents decided not to send me to Cardiff Public High School but to send me to a private high school instead, Cardiff Academy. At first I was disappointed, as I looked forward to attending classes with the people I had previously known from Cardiff public schools. I quickly changed my mind. I felt that Cardiff Academy was a much better choice than Cardiff High School. However, I knew virtually none of the students at Cardiff Academy previously, but took comfort at knowing that few if any knew of the skeletons in my closet.

Fortunately, I quickly progressed academically, though it took a while to make new friends. The guidance counselor, Miss Beauregard, took an interest in me and encouraged me to think positively.

I was very happy to be re-united with my family and my grandmother. I saw Nunna very frequently. Nunna was very relieved to have me back home, as she felt that Genevaville was a breeding ground for criminals.

Since Cardiff Academy was a private school, it was beyond the reach of the ACLU (American Civil

Liberties Union) and other anti-religious organizations as well as being autonomous from the government at any level. For these reasons, attending CA was possibly a lifesaver for me.

Religion up until how had been of limited and only occasional importance in my life. We attended church each Sunday, and we took it seriously to a degree, but it was not a life-changing, transforming force up till now. No one had ever told me that God loved me. Though I gradually gained confidence through my greatly improved academic performance (I made the honor roll every quarter), I felt socially lonely and isolated. There were very few hostile antagonists, though. Seldom did anyone persecute or harass me.

My chemistry teacher, a Pennsylvania Dutchman who had recently moved to New England, had recently become a "born-again" Christian, and I had another class where we studied the Bible somewhat. This chemistry teacher, Mr. Schmidt, attempted with much success to share the Gospel with me. Studying the Bible also caused me to seek answers concerning God and Christ, even though the teachers at my school held a less than traditional high view of the Bible. They were thorough-going evolutionists who claimed that Adam and Eve and the Flood of Noah were "myths," though they held that there were moral messages behind them. They, however, tolerated those who took these "myths" as true.

At the same time, my maternal grandmother Nunna, a dedicated evangelical, was working on me, with increasing success. My paternal grandmother had also been an active Christian. A very faithful Irish-born Catholic, she had unfortunately passed away while I was at Genevaville.

In early February, I decided to give God a chance. I made a deep conversion, and decided to end my vile swearing and greatly reduce my vile speech. Cher's song "Dark Lady" has special meaning to me, as I made my decision only a few days after this song premiered. I started to talk to Mr. Schmidt much about Jesus and the Gospel, and he clearly showed the path. I also began to read the Bible regularly.

Ironically, at this time the other three members of my family had reduced their practice of religion. My mother dropped out of church altogether. The influence of women's libbers, as feminists were called at the time, was a major reason for this, but there were other factors as well. The women's libbers convinced her that religion was invented by "male chauvinists" exclusively for their benefit, and to keep women in their places. She was also greatly offended by the doctrine that every human being is a sinner. I strongly disagree with those who find this doctrine offensive, as it is a totally egalitarian doctrine. It does not discriminate against anyone on the basis of gender, race, nationality, immigration status, social class, "LGBTQ" status, or anything else. The doctrine that every human being is guilty of sin is facing reality. I never questioned it, and never considered it a personal insult. It is necessary that every human being on the individual level confess that he or she is a sinner; otherwise people will not see their need for a Redeemer and Savior in the person of Christ. I fully accepted the doctrine that I was a sinner. Both Mr. Schmidt and Nunna played a significant role in guiding me as a newly dedicated Christian.

Indeed, the doctrine of universal human sinfulness was not only acceptable to me, but even appealed to me considering my cynical nature. It accorded with my experiences in human failings and wickedness. At Genevaville and elsewhere, I saw plenty of empirical evidence that human beings were indeed capable of great evils.

I realize now, however, that there is a need for the great truths of Scripture to be held in balance. Yes, all humans are sinners and need to confess themselves as such. Romans 3:23 teaches that we are all sinners. But we also need to love our neighbor as ourselves and be compassionate and patient and forgiving to our fellow human sinners. There should not be an extreme cynicism, thought there is room for some cynicism. I must forgive the pedophile who molested me on the bus. Christ would demand it.

At this time, my father started attending church less often, and my brother only occasionally.

A light laugh: At Christmas that year my mother told my brother that his father would want him to attend church at least on Christmas. Sam started complaining irreverently, and I responded, "Tomorrow is his birthday. You could be more reverent." Sam then responded, "This kid is getting to be a holy…roller!"

In spring of this school year, I met a minority girl at school (and minorities were very few in New England at that time), and she and I hit it off very well. Shortly there was a spring prom planned, and I had the courage to ask her. She accepted, but her father wanted to meet with my father and me before the dance. The meeting went very well, and my father noted that the difference in race was barely even noticed. Not everyone was happy about it, unfortunately. One girl said, "You're going to the prom with that [deleted] girl Laurie? You'll get married and have racially mixed children." Since I had recently become a born-again Christian I was convinced that God loved all his human creatures, so I quickly rejected whatever racist views I had held previously. I never let it bother me that Laurie was from another race. (Plus, my current girlfriend since 1999 is also a minority!) I feel that there is no place for racism in the heart of any Christian, and that everyone should be evaluated as an individual, and never by group membership.

For several weeks, one of my classes had a substitute teacher. Both she and her husband were devout fundamentalist Baptists. Her husband owned a local gun factory. At the time it seemed incongruous that a dedicated Christian should be involved in such an enterprise. Three decades later, though, conservative Christians would become very strong advocates of private gun ownership. While I support the Constitution including the Second Amendment, I feel that Christians should be much more known for their love of neighbor than a love of guns.

At the prom, Laurie and I were the first couple to get up to dance; what a radical change in my social life!

Laurie truly lit up my life, but we had a disagreement and she broke up with me in early June. However, in late June she called me up and stated that she wanted to get back with me again. We continued to date until early next September.

During my high school years, I remember watching a movie on television entitled something like, *The Family that Nobody Wanted*. This struck me as one of the most heart-warming movies ever. It was about a minister and his wife who adopted numerous unwanted children.

Sadly, I also saw a movie which featured a racially-mixed teenage girl who was rather light-colored, who was ashamed of her mother because of her mother's race. This was a tragic, although accurate, reflection of our highly corrupt and deeply troubling racial history.

Unfortunately, I would not have a steady girlfriend again until the last week of my senior year. This greatly disappointed me.

My social life improved tremendously during my junior year. I made several new friends, especially Ken. My grades continued to climb, and my self-confidence grew steadily.

During my junior year we studied American history. Our teacher convinced me that the greatest hope for social justice is a large middle class. I still agree whole-heartedly.

Then came my senior year. On the second day of the school year, a junior student saw me approaching the guidance counselor's office, and said to me "Your girlfriend is in there." Since I, much to my disappointment, had no girlfriend at the time, I was startled. I then looked into the office and saw a girl who was a total stranger, wearing a cheerleader's uniform. I then said to the junior male student, "She's not my girlfriend. I don't [even] know her."

I had a foreboding that she and I would never get together, that the rumor that she had a crush on me was just a big joke, and that any efforts to bring us together would simply end up giving both of us grief. Since she was obviously a cheerleader and I was not very athletically inclined, (I was on the track team the previous spring though I did poorly) the rumor lacked credibility. Late the previous spring, someone introduced Tracy to me, and she seemed very eager to be introduced to me. I thought for a moment that she may have had a crush on me, but there was not yet sufficient evidence. I never saw her again that year. I thought that this alleged "girlfriend" may have been Tracy, whose appearance remained forgotten to me due to lack of familiarity with her.

I was right; this girl was Tracy. I shortly learned that this was Tracy although she had a radically different hairstyle than she had the previous year.

Several times during the first four weeks of the schoolyear, Tracy greeted me very cordially and enthusiastically. I responded, but with indifference. Several other students also told me that Tracy had a crush on me. I did not want Tracy or those spreading the rumor to think that I was naïve enough to believe the rumor. But Tracy was persistent, and early in the fourth week, I thought, "Tracy keeps being nice to me even though I haven't been nice to her. Maybe I misjudged her. Maybe she really does have a crush on me. From now on I'll be nice to her."

On Friday night the school held a dance. I saw Tracy, and thought "I'll ask her to dance, and depending on how enthusiastically she receives me, I'll ask her for a date. I'll find out for sure if she has a crush on me." So I walked up to Tracy, offered to dance, and she rejected me. I felt that I had been tricked, and that I "let my guard down." I should have known that Tracy's alleged crush on me was a mean-hearted joke, as I first suspected. But at least I learned the truth, and could proceed to follow my crush on another girl, Lisa, who was very beautiful.

For better or for worse, Tracy was not done with me yet. I did not see her again until one-and-one-half week after the dance. Much to my surprise, she was very excited to see me. No one except for relatives had ever greeted me with such excitement. I responded with a mixture of anger, indifference, and then bewilderment. On this occasion, my lack of enthusiasm was justified due to her rejection of me at the dance. A friend of hers then said, "Isn't he cute?" I then smiled cordially; things were occurring so fast.

Any objective by-stander would easily have concluded that Tracy had a crush on me. I suspected that this would have been embarrassing to Tracy, since she obviously stuck out her neck to impress me. If she had not attended the dance, I would have easily become convinced. I was deeply bewildered by the contrasting rejection of me at the dance and her extreme excitement later. I was attending group counseling at the time, and told the two girls in the group about this, and one of them said, "It sounds as if she does have a crush on you. She probably put her friend up to say 'Isn't he cute?' because she wanted you to know about her crush." I then said, "But she rejected me two weeks ago." She then said, "Things have changed since then."

I resolved that I would be nice to Tracy if I encountered her again, though I would not dare to ask her for a date. But our paths did not cross again until next March. I asked her friend in February, (which took much courage) "Does Tracy have a crush on me?" She answered, "I don't think so, not anymore." I dared not ask anything else after that.

In December I asked Lisa for date. We went to a movie, but I do not think that she enjoyed it very much.

When I saw Tracy for the first time in five months, it was evident from her body language that she felt highly uncomfortable at seeing me. She did not look angry or bitter, but highly disappointed. My early prediction that Tracy and I would never have a relationship and that any efforts in that direction would end only in grief for both of us turned out to be highly accurate. Tracy never came to a dance after that one time, and I would not have dared to ask her for a dance (much less a date), if she had.

In February there was a "Sadie Hawkins dance," at which the girls would ask the boys to go to the prom, but no girl asked me. I was very disappointed. Tracy did not ask me, but she did not have a chance to do so since our paths did not cross at that time.

Once during my senior year a freshman student told me that I looked Chinese because I had high cheekbones. I would learn several years later that there was a likelihood that Nunna had some Native American ancestry.

Our biology teacher was a secular Jew, but stated that he had some reservations about evolution, though he did not go into depth with them. Because he was teaching in a private school, he had the freedom to express such a sentiment, without worrying about atheist agitators suing him.

Near Christmas a freshman boy at my high school committed suicide. My mother somehow found out about it, and informed me. I never heard it discussed at school until June, when the Yearbook featured a full-page portrait of him with a message from his sister, a student in her junior year.

Not only did Ken remain a good friend of mine, but his younger sister Linda became a close friend as well. Linda and I got to know each other well in the study hall that we both shared. Ken and I were both active in the Key Club, an organization for high school students that was affiliated with Kiwanis International.

My grades climbed even more. My senior report card was nearly perfect. For each quarter, I earned a 3.8 average, but each quarter the single "B" was in a different course, and I ended up with a 4.0 average for each semester and for the whole year.

Now the end of the year, and graduation, were approaching. I suddenly and painfully realized that I was not nearly as popular as I thought, nor was I nearly as well-respected student as I had thought. I suddenly worried that once I graduated I would lose all of my friends, which turned out to be an unnecessary worry, though I did lose most of my academic and social confidence. At the graduation ceremony, I did not receive a single scholarship, award, or even any mention for academic performance. I felt that all my efforts had been a waste, and quickly lost my motivation.

I usually rode my bicycle to school, but on a Thursday my bicycle had a flat tire, so I had to walk. This would be fantastically providential. Because of this, my friend Ken and his sister Linda gave me a ride home. Ken knew that I was disappointed that I would not be likely to attend the senior prom, so he suggested in Linda's presence, "Why don't you take Linda to the prom?" Linda suddenly became highly ecstatic! I decided to give the suggestion a chance.

Linda bought a special dress for the occasion. I picked her up, and her parents told us that she could stay out as late as she wished. This was one of the happiest nights of our lives for both of us. I did not bring Linda home until after midnight. Linda and I dated for about two years, and both she and her brother Ken remained close friends to me.

Despite my worries to the contrary, I had a decent social life that summer. But I was quickly losing my self-confidence, both academic and social, and was spiraling downward quickly.

Making things worse was my summer job at a local athletic field. I did not enjoy the work very much, and my co-workers treated my very condescendingly. I did not become mentally depressed, but my enthusiasm for life was disappearing very quickly. It would take decades to get it back. However, it eventually happened.

CHAPTER FIVE
The College Years

My four years on campus were almost entirely disappointing. I attended a college about 12 miles from my home in Cardiff. My immediate concern was my social life, along with fears that I would not fit in with the students unless I drank alcoholic beverages heavily. At that time, the legal drinking age was 18, and alcohol was nearly everywhere.

I was assigned a roommate, but he was a smoker. I had stated on my application that I had a preference for a non-smoking roommate. That evening there was a so-called "freshman mixer," to help new students meet other new students, but it was not helpful to me.

My roommate wanted to be with students that he knew better, so he moved elsewhere and I was assigned an older student, Eric. Since Eric was a born-again Christian, I was eagerly looking forward to having him as a roommate. However, he was authoritarian and domineering, and often criticized me in front of others. I quickly became disappointed with him, but at least he did not drink alcohol, or smoke, and was not sexually active.

I joined the university's Christian Fellowship. In some ways it was very helpful. I made many acquaintances and a few friends there. One member who was a truly saintly person who later became a closer friend was Mark. He had accepted Christ rather recently, and took seriously the commands of the Gospel. He is now a nationally-recognized ichthyologist (one who studies fish). Mark was the son of a minister in a mainline Protestant denomination, one which was even at the time regarded as one of the most liberal. Mark questioned if his father, though a minister, was a true Christian. Mark clearly rejected whatever liberal theological influence had existed in his mind, and became a stalwart faithful Christian. He is possibly the finest, saintliest evangelical I have ever known.

College was highly disappointing in every way.

My high school chemistry teacher, Mr. Schmidt, had a part-time job as a caretaker at a local home for badly handicapped children, which could be boring as it was in the late evening, when he had nothing to do except watch out for incidents that might happen, but seldom did. He let me call him late on Friday or Saturday night, and he remained a good friend and tried to give me spiritual and other encouragement.

I called my grandmother and Linda every night. I seldom called my parents, though.

I attended weekly Bible studies. Unfortunately, I had fallen into deep self-pity, and a rather pervasive one at that. Though I believed intensely in the doctrines of traditional, biblical Christianity (such as the Virgin Birth, the Trinity, the Atonement, the Resurrection of Jesus, grace, and universal human sinfulness), my belief that God loved me was rather weak. I was not grateful for the blessings that I had, due to my strong degree of self-pity. I was aware that multitudes of leaders in the mainline churches embraced evolution and dismissed Adam and Eve and the Flood as "myths," but was blissfully unaware that many of them also rejected many of these other doctrines. My self-pity distorted nearly everything in my life. I thought that many people looked down upon me who did nothing of the sort. And it would not be until over thirty years later that I would learn that I was autistic, which was not the fault of any of the students or faculty at the university.

I went home nearly every weekend. I would visit Ken, and go on a date with Linda. Since campus was only 12 miles from Cardiff, I called Linda almost every night. Without Ken and Linda I would have found it very difficult if not impossible to have made it through the first two years of college.

Academically, I floundered. I thought that I might be interested in journalism, but I earned only a "C" in my journalism class, so I gave up on journalism. I did poorly in mathematics, so I dropped my math course. This left me with only four classes. I earned one other "C" and two "A's." One of the courses was in "Honors." The professor was an avowed infidel, and two days were devoted to the theory, attributed by many to Albert Schweitzer, that the "historic" Jesus bore little resemblance to the Jesus of the Bible. The professor denied the Resurrection of Jesus, and claimed that Bible scholars admitted that the original texts of the Gospels contained no Resurrection story. (I would later learn that liberal "Christian" scholars used the argument that since "Q" contained no references to the Resurrection, the Resurrection was a "myth" later added to the text, but this argument is based upon a theory upon a theory upon a theory that was never proved. I explained this in my earlier book.) I did not allow any of this to weaken my faith in Christ or the Bible.

I earned a 3.0 average my first semester, though I was disappointed that I got two "C's." The second semester was far worse. I earned only a 2.25 average, and my academic self-confidence spiraled down very fast.

A truly positive change was attendance at a Catholic charismatic meeting each Sunday night. The unofficial leader was Alden, whom I deeply respected and admired as a deeply saintly, devoted Christian who was highly enthusiastic for Jesus and the Scriptures. He was filled with love and compassion for nearly everyone. He had little religious upbringing; he came from one of the most heavily unchurched counties in the country, where very few people attended church. This weekly prayer meeting, where the Bible and the name of Jesus were so prevalent, rejuvenated me weekly. I loved it! I regarded the charismatic movement as a progressive movement in the truest sense of the word.

Eric and I agreed that we should not continue as roommates for another year, and I moved in with Bill as my roommate.

I got along well with Bill, and learned a great deal about the Bible from him. He was my roommate again for my third year on campus, then he graduated.

Concerning my Christian friends and acquaintances in college, I shall add this: I saw no evidence of racism or racial or ethnic prejudice among them. They even repudiated such. They believed in equal pay for equal work and equal individual opportunity, but beyond that they were mostly unsupportive of feminism. Many were strongly opposed to women's ordination.

Though I would certainly not say that all of them were free from all forms of hypocrisy, I much respected them for having much higher morals than the vast majority of students. For the most part, they never got drunk and they faithfully abstained from sex out-of-wedlock. They felt that high morals were integral to being a Christian. They were overwhelmingly opposed to homosexuality and the gay liberation movement. Ironically, Kendall, a male Christian student from a strict evangelical sect, came out as gay three decades later, but none of us ever suspected that he was gay.

During my second year I decided to try business as a major (we did not actually declare majors until our junior year), but did poorly in my accounting class. I took the class again the second semester, and was the best student in my class! I may have had a successful career in accounting, but my instructor for an intermediate class in accounting ruined whatever chances I had. He was the worst teacher ever, and had extremely poor teaching skills. In our first class of the semester, he said, "There are two types of accounting, financial accounting and managerial accounting. Managerial accounting is…uh…it's accounting…" I had him for a subsequent class and he once said to two students in the back row, "You two students are talking too much. You need to separate a little." One of them got up and left the room saying, "Are were far enough apart now?" The other students loved it!

The second year ended, and I returned home for the summer. When my father pick me up to go home, he informed me that my mother had recently seen an attorney to start divorce proceedings. Though this was a disappointment, I was not surprised. Dad informed me that he would be moving out shortly, and would have to find a new home.

Linda and I went to her senior prom, and had a wonderful time. She was planning to move to California to attend college, so I knew that we would not be together for much longer.

Shortly afterwards Linda and I went to a nearby lake, and on the way home we heard Barry Manilow's new song "Copacabana" for the first time. When we were nearly home, Linda told me that she was breaking up with me; she was unwilling to wait until the end of the summer. I was very sad about this and for the next few weeks the song "Copacabana" reminded me of our last few minutes together.

I never saw Linda again. However, she wrote to me shortly after she arrived in California, and we spoke on the telephone at Thanksgiving. She wrote to me at Christmas. I wrote back, including the lines, "I was surprised to have heard from you again. I thought that by now you hated my guts." A few days later, Linda's mother telephoned me. She said, "Something in your letter to Linda has her really upset. Can you remember what you said that could have got her so upset? She thinks of you as her best friend." I could easily surmise what got Linda so upset. It was these two lines, but I did not want to admit it to her mother, so I said, "I don't know what it was," though in fact I did know. Linda wrote me again after the end of the year. I wrote back, but that was the last time that we ever communicated with each other.

During her first semester on campus, Linda met her new boyfriend, an Australian immigrant. Shortly afterward, she was diagnosed with Hodgkin's disease. Her boyfriend treated her with much compassion during her ordeal, and Linda survived. They got married in 1983, which did not bother me one bit. Her brother Ken had a very difficult time dealing with Linda's illness. He was very fearful that she would die. He flunked out of college that semester because he did not take his final exams, and was suspended for a semester.

This double whammy of Linda's breakup with me and my parents' approaching divorce took a strong toll on me. It made me far more cynical about marriage and even about relationships, and about people in general. I was not "hot to trot" to find a new girlfriend, and concluded that I would probably never get married. I became much more lonely and isolated. It would be nearly 19 years before I would even go on another date, and over 20 years before I would have another girlfriend. I had also concluded that the opposite sex did not find me attractive or even suitable for dating, let alone marriage. I had concluded that no girl at Cardiff Academy found me attractive or suitable, and with Linda's sudden breakup with me, I lost interest in dating or having a girlfriend. However, I did not feel any attraction to the gay lifestyle or have any gay feelings.

Ken and Linda were two of the best friends that I ever had, and I deeply regret the tremendous grief that I must have given them due to my loss of sociability resulting from my anger, extreme self-pity, bitterness toward life, and extreme cynicism about life and people in general. They deserved far better from a friend than I gave.

I attended college and lived on campus for the fourth year. My roommate Ron was very easily to get along with, and was also a dedicated Christian.

I was seriously considering becoming a clergyman. One reason is because it was a field where being unmarried would be acceptable. This choice would turn out to be disastrous.

Though this was my fourth year on campus, I was far from graduating. My grade point accumulated average was approximately 2.05, and I had far fewer course than needed for a diploma. I decided to drop out of college, to return later.

My mother was profoundly disappointed with my decision, and my grandmother somewhat so.

Because of my interest in the ministry, I attended a summer event for young people considering ordination in Cambridge, Massachusetts. It would prove to be a keen disappointment. There were two clergymen at the event, along with four laymen who had considered the ministry. I got along well with Larry, though we disagreed strongly on theology and the Bible. Until now I had had little contact with liberal theology and liberal biblical scholarship. I knew that liberals ridiculed Adam and Eve, the Flood, Jonah and the Whale, and possibly Job as "myths," but beyond that I had little contact with liberal theology. Larry tried hard to convince me to believe in evolution, to no avail. He constantly showed off his knowledge of "modern scholarship" by saying irreverent things about the Bible. He claimed that Moses' parting of the water was "myth," and that Jesus never said much of what the four Evangelists attributed to him. In particular, he loudly claimed, "You know when Jesus said, 'Thou art Peter and on this Rock I will build my church?' Well, all scripture scholars say that Jesus never said that!"

I knew that this statement was a falsehood. I knew that there were hundreds of conservative and evangelical biblical scholars who believed in a high view of the inspiration and reliability of Scripture, and that what Larry said was a view of only a minority (though this minority represented the vast majority of those in the "mainline" churches.)

One of the other participants was an enthusiastic charismatic named Victor. He was very proud of being half-Jewish and half-Italian.

On one occasion we had a small service, and Larry preached the sermon. And what was the Gospel passage, but one in which Peter said to Jesus, "Thou art the Christ, the Son of the Living God!" Larry could not resist the opportunity to show off his knowledge of "modern scholarship," and said, "Here we have Peter expressing a belief in Jesus as the Son of God. Well, scripture scholars say that no one believed that Jesus was the Son of God until after the Resurrection. So the Scriptures here are not historically reliable."

That night, four of us went to Boston. One person said, "I could tell that Lucien and Victor, our two Fundamentalists, were not too happy with some of Larry's comments." Then Victor said, "I thought Lucien was going to get up and say, 'You must be born again!'" All of us found this hilarious!

Ironically, Larry's comment about Peter's recognition of Jesus as the Son of God is relatively orthodox compared to what many liberal clergy would say. At least Larry believed in the Resurrection. Many, if not a majority, of theological liberals deny the Resurrection of Jesus. However, Larry was willing to live in peace with our disagreements, and was highly tolerant for a theological liberal.

The other minister, Peter, was often irreverent at times. He once said, "Jesus' contemporaries must have said, 'Who does this crazy carpenter think he is, God?'" and "There was a car with the bumper sticker, 'Honk if you love Jesus!' and the motorist behind him then passed him and shouted to him, [obscenity deleted]!'"

After this summer, I had deep misgivings about the possibility of entering the ministry, but I continued to believe deep down that such was what I really wanted. I thought that I could "infiltrate" a largely liberal ministry as a conservative, orthodox believer.

CHAPTER SIX
Early Adulthood

I returned to Cardiff to live with my mother and brother. My parents' divorce was nearly final. My father had moved into a new mobile home in a new park. The mobile home was large and technologically advanced by the standards of the time.

I tried to make the times in Cambridge sound much more positive than they really were. But shortly afterwards my mother, grandmother and I met at my grandmother's house and I let them know my true feelings. Both my mother and grandmother were disappointed. My mother said that many people had become disillusioned with churches in recent years, especially the "Congregational Church" [The United Church of Christ], and the [United] Methodist Church. She said, "The clergy preach one thing and practice another," and referred to the arrogance of the clergy. They also gathered that much of what was preached at the summer event was akin to communism.

I would need to find a job, but had no luck in finding one. I did not actually try that hard. I had no confidence in my ability to find a job or to impress any potential employer. I also knew that most employees required tons of "experience" which few applicants in their early twenties could provide.

My mother would say to me early on many mornings that she wanted me to get up early and look for a job. I once ridiculed her as saying, "I want you to get up, I want you to get out of bed, I want you to put on your clothes, I want you to go out, and I want you to look for a job." This annoyed her.

The only real effort that I made toward employment was to take a course at the local H. & R. Block tax preparer. I studied and attended classes.

By early November my mother was quickly losing patience with me in my failure to get a job. Then, my father and Nunna (his former mother-in-law) met to discuss the possibility of my moving in with Nunna. My father offered Nunna $20.00 a week for a year for room and board. Nunna was very agreeable to the idea. She expressed strong disappointment with her daughter in "kicking me" out of her home. She said referring to me, "He's such a good boy. He's not in trouble with the law, or guzzling beer!" I thought it was hilarious that Nunna implied in front of my father that beer was undesirable, since my father drank beer nearly every day. My grandmother held many traditional Yankee Puritan values, and her ancestors would have been proud of her.

Next week, I moved in with Nunna. We enjoyed living with each other tremendously, though it took a few days to get used to it.

Nunna wore eyeglasses with very large frames, and I saw her several times without her glasses, and noticed something very interesting about her. I thought that she looked so sweet without her glasses. I said to her, "[The way your face curves outward next to your eyes] looks so sweet!" She then said, "You like high cheekbones." I then said, "[How can] you have high cheekbones? You're not an Indian." She then said, "I have them." [I intend no racial slurs; I feel that my grandmother's high cheekbones were a highly beautiful feature; high cheekbones are my favorite facial feature on women, though I realize that "high cheekbones" have a strong racial connotation.]

Even though Nunna did not believe much that she read in the tabloids, she subscribed to two or three of them. I remember one story in one of them about a Vietnamese girl from a very poor family, who abandoned her in a wooden box, who fortunately was adopted by an American family. Many years later, I would meet a young woman whose fate started out similarly. More on that to come.

Fortunately, I got a part-time job preparing tax returns, though I knew that the job was by nature seasonal, and my performance was mediocre. The business sent me to its location at a nearby department store. When tax season was over, I applied for a job at this store. Fortunately, I was hired on the spot. I was given a job as a cashier at the store's appliance parts and repair department. I spent most of my time on my feet for the first few months, but several months later my boss decided to place me at a desk waiting on customers on the telephone and performing inventory control. This was far more agreeable to me. The job was part-time; typically I worked 30 to 32 hours weekly, though I occasionally worked for 40 hours. There were no part-time benefits but all employees could contribute to and receive benefits from the company's profit-sharing program. I enjoyed this job far better than my previous jobs doing grounds maintenance in the summers, and I enjoyed it far more than attending college.

Shortly later I returned to college on a part-time basis, taking only one or two courses at a time, but did poorly.

Shortly before this time, the Christian Right movement had begun, and it was alleged that this movement gave Ronald Reagan the swing votes that he needed from the large evangelical minority that he needed to win the presidency in 1980. Jerry Falwell was a major founder and leader of the Christian Right, and shortly became the victim of extreme scorn and outright hatred by secular and religious liberals. The

Christian Right proclaimed that secular liberals, the liberally-dominated U.S. Supreme Court, the liberally-biased news media, secular humanism, the welfare state, and liberals in general were to blame for the decline of morality and religious influence, increased crime, attacks on the institutions of marriage and family, and multitudes of social evils. The Christian Right regarded the proposed ERA (Equal Rights Amendment) to the U.S. Constitution as a potential threat to the institutions of family and marriage and religious freedom. The proposed ERA was supposedly to guarantee equal rights regardless of sex (now usually called "gender.") Christian Right activists were largely responsible for defeating the ERA.

During this time Nunna and I regularly viewed the *700 Club,* hosted by Pat Robertson. He convinced me that the American Civil Liberties Union, which he frequently denounced at the time, was the fiercest and most relentless enemy of religious freedom in America. I quickly regarded it as a satanic organization, and also regarded many of its stands not only as antireligious but antidemocratic and elitist and grossly amoral and immoral as well. Rightly or wrongly, I considered it Public Enemy Number One.

In autumn of 1981, I traveled to the Boston area for a few days. While I was there, I telephoned Alden, whom I had known from the charismatic meeting four years earlier, and whom I had so much admired as a saintly person eager to share Christ's love with others. He had been studying for the ministry since 1978. Unfortunately, I was deeply disappointed and disillusioned with what I heard from him. The ministerial training was highly liberal, deeply into higher criticism of the Bible, anti-Americanism, and even some Marxism. Those in training had ruined his potential, and had made him vehemently opposed to much of what he formerly believed. He repeatedly insisted that higher criticism was the only "legitimate scholarship," and even accused people of using religion as an "escape," (echoes of Marxism) and had accepted liberation theology. He stated that those who use religion as an escape may as well "hit the bottle." This was highly offensive, because religion brings benefits both the individual and society; drunkenness is dangerous to both. He even seemed to suggest that Americans deserved to lose some human rights because of their opposition to Marxism and communism, and denounced the Peace Corps as a front for the United States government to gain information about potential communist uprisings in the Third World. He even said, "Russia once agreed to disarm its nuclear weapons, but we 'had to fight communism.'" (I cannot prove or disprove this assertion.) He regarded opposition to communism as a major threat to world peace, but did not seem to regard communism and Marxism as threats to world peace or human rights.

About this time I was becoming suspicious of what I could easily see as a double standard on human rights on the part of mainline churches and their leaders, coupled with anti-Americanism. There was constant condemnation of human rights violations in El Salvador, Guatemala, Chile, Argentina, and South Korea, along with blaming the Yankee Imperialists for these violations, while there was silence regarding human rights violations in the Soviet Union, North Korea, Cuba, Poland, Czechoslovakia, China and other communist nations. Many of these activists constantly denounced United States opposition to the spread of Marxism and communism as "immoral," and they were highly dogmatic and opinionated about this, while failing to denounce violence, destruction of property, guerrilla warfare, and terrorism on the part of Marxists and communists as such. Even the liberally-inclined news media seemed unsympathetic toward Third World Marxist movements, and reported about violence, terrorism, and destruction of crops and other property by Marxist guerrillas and terrorists in Central America. Some church activists even exalted the Marxist Sandinistas of Nicaragua and Marxist warriors, agitators and terrorists in El Salvador as "prophets of God's Kingdom." Some were even claiming that the United States was the world's biggest exporter of human rights violations, and gave the greatest amount of foreign aid to the six or so worse violators in the world. This seemed like little more than falsehood and one-sided Marxist propaganda, as the worst violators of human rights in the world were communist nations, toward which the USA was immensely hostile, and vice versa.

Being now far more mature and with the aid of hindsight, I realize that such nations as El Salvador, Guatemala, and Chile were severe violators of human rights at the time, and that maybe the United States government should have responded far differently than it did. Had the critics of United States foreign policy been equally critical of the foreign policies of communist nations, they may have convinced me that the USA was indeed mistaken. Had they condemned Marxist-sponsored terrorism and intervention instead of having a double standard, they may have convinced me. But at the time they seemed like little more than puppets of Marxism.

In spring of 1983, Nunna's health began to decline ominously. Earlier in the year she went to a nearby hospital for three days for an operation. She kept it secret from all relatives; a friend took her to the hospital and brought her home. She told us that she went to Danvers, Massachusetts to visit a relative. We learned the truth two months later. Her health declined still further and I was disappointed when my mother told me that she would likely die before Christmas.

In May she needed around-the-clock attention. This was divided between other relatives, me, and various nurse's aides. To make things even worse, I broke my wrist when I placed on the brakes while riding my bicycle; it immediately stopped and threw me to the ground, landing on my right wrist. This made it harder to help Nunna when she needed help. Once she asked me to crush a pill to make it easier to swallow, but I was unable to do so.

Nunna was very courageous in facing her death. She was in immense pain. Her typical New England value of self-sufficiency made it more painful for her to be so dependent on others. She even said, "I'll go when God takes me, and I wish he'd take me tonight."

At 11:50 on May 31, 1983, the loud phlegmatic sound that her breathing made suddenly disappeared. I suspected that she had expired. I quickly got out of bed, and confirmed that this had happened. The nurse's aide, who typically arrived at midnight, was ten minutes late, and I told her what happened.

I called my mother and my uncle, and they quickly arrived. My uncle called the local funeral director, and he arrived with his hearse. He confirmed her death, placed her in the hearse, and took her away. By now it was 2:00 a.m.

I took Nunna's death surprisingly well, and relatives felt that I did, though it was a tremendous disappointment and loss. At least she lived several years longer than my mother predicted many years earlier.

For the next month, I continued to live in Nunna's home, but I had to move out shortly, and moved to an apartment near the slums. When I moved in, the reality of Nunna's death sank in far more deeply. My cost of living increased immensely, with no immediate source of increased income. I had to reconsider my future, as well as attending college full-time. I was now reconsidering entering the ministry, and went to meet with a clergyman about it. I obviously did not make a good first impression, but in subsequent meetings I made a much mellower impression, and was eventually accepted to a seminary and clerical formation. I went back to college full-time while continuing to work, changed my major to philosophy, and graduated in late 1984.

Fortunately in late October of 1983 my father allowed me to live with him in his mobile home. My brother had lived in the extra bedroom, but went back to college, and a different college, in September, thus vacating the room. I was very happy about moving in with my father, as I no longer had to pay rent.

I returned to college full time in early 1984. I took five courses in philosophy, including some in theology. One of these courses was about higher criticism of the Bible or the "historical critical method." The professor of this class used the typical argument that modern biblical criticism was the result of the "enlightenment," but admitted that it was a "secular approach to a sacred book." He argued that biblical criticism was "unbiased" because it was not influenced by traditional, historic Christian doctrine. I commented, though, that interpreting the Bible according to modern philosophy was a bias. He responded, "Guilty as charged," as he could not find any other answer to my challenge. This professor, though, did have a pleasing personality and was far less opinionated and dogmatic than the usual theology professor, who fortunately for me was on a one-year sabbatical. He was, however, highly critical of me for using the word "supernatural," and for my refusal to stop using it. Nonetheless, he otherwise treated me very fairly and gave me high grades.

The usual theology professor returned the next semester. He was highly arrogant, condescending, and disrespectful toward those who disagreed with him. He was so arrogant that he even refused to follow the university's protocol in giving us a chance at the end of the semester to fill out the proper evaluation forms. He even once said, "When I hear people say, 'God loves you' and 'Jesus loves you,' it is so sickeningly sentimental. I just want to throw up." Is this how the partisans of liberal theology view God's love?

When I returned to college in autumn 1984, I noticed a remarkable change among the professors and instructors. This was when "political correctness" suddenly erupted, and when it became very obvious, and suddenly so, that a highly authoritarian, dogmatic, and intolerant atmosphere would now be the norm on college campuses; and the news media, other institutions, and the mainline churches quickly fell into subservience to political correctness and became zealous enforcers of it. Though political correctness was not so named until circa 1991, it was already very much evident. This meant that there would be no dissent from the liberal party line on issues relating to various issues, especially gender issues. Those who dissented must keep their feelings to themselves, or see their potential livelihoods and careers destroyed. My first encounter with political correctness was when I took a course during my last semester concerning ethnic and cultural diversity and conflict. My teacher had outstanding teaching skills, one of the most outstanding teachers I ever had in that regard. Unfortunately, he was highly dogmatic and intolerant about gender issues. He said early in the semester that he would not tolerate any "sexist language" in his class or on written material submitted by students. I saw this as an attack on free speech. Though feminism, or "women's lib" as it was previously called, had caused intense conflict within my family, I had never regarded it as totalitarian, but I now began to see it as such. Under political correctness, anything labeled as "sexist" or "sexist language" would not be tolerated in the name of free speech or political or religious freedom, nor was it up to the individual to decide for oneself what is or is not "sexist." This decision was for the politically correct censors and zealots alone to decide.

I soon concluded that the defeat of the ERA was a tremendous victory for religious freedom and freedom of speech. Having recently detected totalitarian elements in both radical feminism and political correctness, it would be easy to predict that if the ERA were ratified, the ACLU, politically correct enforcers, and other enemies of religious freedom would have a very powerful tool to use. The feminists and enemies of religious freedom could allege that any church or congregation that used "sexist language" in its liturgies, Bible translations, its hymns, its preaching, which called God "Father," or Jesus the "Son" of God or "Son" of "Man," or which refused to ordain women, or which opposed a woman's "right to choose" abortion, was operating in violation of the ERA, and should be forced to close by the authorities, or made subject to state discrimination. I am not accusing the ACLU in particular of any of these actions, but sensing the ACLU's fierce and intense hostility to religion I would never trust them with my religious freedom, or anyone else's. Bear in mind that the ERA would be as much of the Constitution as the First Amendment, and opponents of religious freedom could argue that the First Amendment does not protect anything that violates the ERA. In addition, most secular humanists hold an unhistorical or historically false interpretation of the First Amendment that is hostile to religion and morality.

Then there is the real though unacknowledged problem that the term "equality" is highly and dangerously ambiguous. Does "equality" mean that all *individuals,* regardless of race or gender have equal rights to be free from discrimination, or does it mean equal *collective outcomes,* meaning that women must be guaranteed half of all the upper-middle-class and upper-class and elite careers and the exact same per capita income as white men, even if this means discrimination against white men? In other words, does it mean that a white male individual should have the same individual rights as an individual woman or individual minority member, or that a white male individual must be penalized by antimale discrimination because of what *other* white male individuals have done? For example, if a white male individual applies to medical school, should he be penalized because fewer than half of all doctors are female? And take the issue that women must be guaranteed the exact same per capita income as men, an implied demand of the "76 cent" agitation which is constantly rammed down our throats by the news media and other outlets, feminists, many college professors and journalists, many mainline church leaders, and various politicians. *I believe intensely and unreservedly in equal pay for EQUAL work.* This "76 cent" statistic ignores the facts that women work fewer hours per capita than men, that many male-dominated occupations pay more because are highly dangerous and hazardous to health, and that the top 1% of men skew upward the average male per capital income. This "76 cent" statistic is not based on comparing men and women who are truly comparable. For in-depth documentation, I refer the reader to Chapter 5 of my earlier book, *Toward a Balanced Message.* I feel that it is highly unjust if not immoral to penalize and punish lower-income men for what higher-income men have done, but obviously the feminists and politically-correct liberals feel otherwise. Most feminists and politically correct enforcers feel that discrimination against men should not be considered "discrimination." Many mainline "social justice" activists have long thought that anything that promotes the feminist agenda promotes social justice, is "prophetic" and promotes God's

Kingdom, which strikes me as highly naïve and reflects a lack of true concern for social justice as well as a lack of discernment and critical, analytical thinking.

A few opponents of the ERA argued that there were already sufficient laws to prohibit discrimination based on gender and to require equal pay for equal work; therefore, the more legitimate demands of moderate feminists were already guaranteed. There was no need for a new Constitutional amendment to guarantee what was already the law of the land.

It took very little time for political correctness to spread beyond college campuses to the mainstream media and to the mainline churches. I quickly sensed intense propagation and enforcement of political correctness and its rigid dogmas in my own denomination, and to a lesser extent, in my own local church. And conformity to politically correct thought and speech codes was not sufficient; everyone and every institution had to make feminism a high priority, if not the highest priority of all.

In the fall of 1984, a poster appeared in the library at my college. It announced that Rosemary Reuther, whom I call the "dean" of feminist theologians, would give a speech at my college. The poster read, "Can a male savior save women?" I immediately though of a book that I had read four years earlier, suggesting a connection between the elimination of "sexism" by religious leaders and a denial of the Incarnation, the essential Christian doctrine that God became incarnate as a human being in the person of Jesus. The immensely horrifying thought entered my mind that before much longer the feminists would deny the Incarnation as a "sexist" doctrine, and that the humanity of Jesus would be repudiated in order to deny his masculinity, and that the leaders of the mainline churches, who were increasingly becoming overzealous enforcers of radical feminism and political correctness, would fall into place by rejecting the Incarnation. In fairness, I cannot ascertain Reuther's own beliefs concerning the Incarnation, and am not accusing her of denying this doctrine, though I definitely do not regard her as a prophet. I would later recall that 2 John 7 identifies the antichrist with a denial of the Incarnation. This, plus the rapidly increasing tendency of the mainline churches to treat radical Feminism as an absolute, made me immensely fearful. Somehow, however, I felt confident that I could infiltrate a mainline denomination and remain orthodox and faithful to biblical Christianity.

My local church had recently hired a new director of religious education. He was not too well received by the congregation. He received criticism when he said that the sin of Sodom had nothing to do with homosexuality, and even more when he said that nothing supernatural ever occurs and has ever occurred. When someone objected, "What about the Resurrection of Jesus?" he responded that that was the only supernatural thing that ever occurred and the only exception to the rule. He also insisted that the burning bush was a "myth," which seems to be a major dogma among liberals.

I learned in April of 1985 that I had been accepted to ministerial formation, and was highly pleased. I had needed letters of recommendation from those knowledgeable of my intellectual and spiritual capacities. The theology professor that I had earlier graciously agreed, though he did not hesitate to "criticize me for using theological terms that are obsolete," obviously a reference to my persistent use of the term "supernatural" that irritated him so much. I suspect that liberal theologians seek to eliminate this term because most of them no longer believe that anything supernatural occurs, can occur, or has occurred; most of them do not even believe that God is supernatural. Liberals, my God is bigger than your god!

I arrived at the seminary in late August. I was not there long before I noticed that the same obsession with and rigid enforcement of political correctness was prevalent there. A day never occurred when someone did not have to change several words in the prayers or liturgy because someone claimed that they were "sexist." We were constantly harangued about the evils of "sexism."

I had and have never been to any institution any more male-dominated numerically than the seminary. But I had and have never been to any institution where antimale sentiment was nearly as strong and intense as this seminary. The powers there wanted us to hate ourselves for being male.

But an ever bigger problem to me was the other liberal twists in both theology and biblical studies. We were quickly greeted with the questionable claim that we must interpret the Bible in accord with the teachings of the "enlightenment," which was held in great reverence at the seminary. As argued in my earlier book, there were many truly Christian leaders and intellectuals within the enlightenment, so the claim that all the leaders of the enlightenment were antisupernatural is highly debatable, but most "young skulls full of mush" did not know any better.

It is likely that a large minority of both students and faculty were gay or lesbian (or, in today's lingo, LGBTQ). I strongly suspect that this was much of the reason for the extreme emphasis on feminism and other politically correct issues. Being a radical, dogmatic feminist was a subtle though "respectable" way for gay men to assert themselves.

One major view at the seminary was the assertion of "black-and-white thinking is evil and everything is gray." However, when there was any issue related to gender or other issue about which the people at the seminary were dogmatic, everything was as black-and-white as possible and there was no gray.

My best friend at the seminary was Fred, and I doubt that I would have made it through the first semester without him. We continue to stay in contact.

Another really big issue, though, was the personal problems caused by autism, and God was the only being in the universe at the time who knew that I was on the autistic spectrum. The faculty were immensely and relentlessly critical of me for my alleged lack of social skills and the resulting social awkwardness.

Many of us once attended a retreat at a center in Maryland. While we were there, a group of women from an African Methodist Church had rented some rooms for a retreat. We had little contact with them, but once I was walking past their rented room when the door was opened, and I was struck by the deep joy and enthusiasm of these women. Here were three dozen or so women only two decades after the Civil Rights Movement, and likely every one of them had been victimized deeply by racial hatred, prejudice, and conflict. Despite this, they had a deep inner peace and joy that could not be destroyed. They made a big impact on me. I deeply regret that I do not have the solution for our four-century long mistreatment of African-Americans (Blacks) and Native Americans (Indians), and no one else seems to have the answers either. We must admit our abject failures, seek God's forgiveness while humbly acknowledging our faults, and love our neighbor as ourselves regardless of race or nationality. [I feel strongly that the effort to promote social justice for ALL will require input from a vast DIVERSITY of viewpoints and input from men and women of all races, ethnicities, faiths, AND social and economic classes. The Politically Correct concept of "diversity" means men and women of all races, social classes, LGBTQ's, and ethnicities enforcing the same simplistic Politically Correct propaganda and censoring and intimidating any viewpoints otherwise. Feminists would seek to exclude most WOMEN who do not share their upper-middle-class and upper-class values, which frankly is classist. If lower-income "white males" were encouraged to share their views, maybe they would be far less attracted to "right-wing" politics.]

One day at our worship service, one of the professors denounced or at least watered down the doctrine of the atonement, the doctrine that the death of Christ on the cross satisfied God's demand for justice against the sins of humanity. He claimed that this doctrine "limited" God's mercy and that for this reason theologians were increasingly rejecting it. I thought, "What absolutely poor theology! It was the atonement which satisfied God's demand for justice and made it possible for God's mercy to be extended to the Gentiles." Before long it became evident that liberal theologians were involved in an effort to deny Jesus' atonement for human sin by his death on the cross. Not even once during my two years at the seminary did any professor assert an orthodox, biblical view of the atonement. One of my professors issued his own notebook, and among his notes was an attack on the atonement, with the pathetic argument, "Doesn't this limit God's mercy?" He also assigned a book by a prominent Australian theologian noting that belief in the atonement among theologians has "fallen on hard times," also using the now usual but highly pathetic and invalid liberal argument that it "seems to limit God's mercy."

Another big disappointment in liberal theology is that it motivates people to be concerned for "social justice" but does not deliver it, and promotes immense fallacies and highly simplistic analyses and solutions. My earlier book dealt with this in much depth and detail. Liberal theology blames "social structures" and discrimination for virtually all poverty and social problems, but ignores the role that personal sin plays in causing poverty and personal failure. The simplistic assertion that "sexism" is the world's greatest evil and cause of problems was constantly rammed down our throats, but on only one occasion did anyone ever condemn greed, and even on that one occasion the criticism was weak. In my earlier book I explained the concepts of internalism and externalism and the role that both play in causing social evils. *Internalism* is the view that one's own failures, poor judgments, and weaknesses are the major cause of poverty, while *externalism* is the view that unjust social structures and discrimination cause nearly all poverty and social problems. I feel that there is a need for a *balance* between both of these, and that purely to hold one or the other is both simplistic and dangerous. I also explained, with biblical support, that greed is wicked and an obstacle to God's kingdom (Ephesians 5:5), but the seminary leaders felt that greed promoted social justice and equality if a woman or other member of an "oppressed" group practiced it. I feel that any truly Christian social justice activist should be "ramming" Ephesians 5:5 (which condemns greed as a form of idolatry which will keep its practitioners from having any share in the kingdom of Christ and of God) down people's throats, instead of the "76 cent" fallacy.

Their approach to social justice, though typical of the mainline churches, was highly inadequate and disappointing. Unlike many of my fellow theologically conservative Christians, I feel that Christians should indeed be concerned about social justice, but as a *supplement* to the doctrines and priorities of traditional, biblical Christianity and not as a *substitute* for them. The seminary's leadership also seemed to feel that upper-class women were God's favorite people, as they placed an extreme emphasis on their interests while ignoring the working class. I feel that a biblical approach to social justice does indeed exist, and made an intricate attempt to develop such an approach in my earlier book, *Toward a Balanced Message.*

One of the greatest hypocrisies of all was their double standard of who is most entitled to the benefits of being the image of God. The doctrine that every human being is created in the image of God is almost universally accepted by Christians of all types, but liberals seemed to apply this doctrine inconsistently. They would be quick to point out that members of groups that liberals favor are the image of God, while ignoring that white males, conservatives, and other members of groups that they disfavor are equally the image of God. They would allege that an upper-class woman has the right to earn dozens of times the average per capita income because she was the image of God (as though upper-class people are any more God's image than the poor), while being silent about the verbal abuse by feminists and politically correct agitators against white males. As I see it, an upper-class woman or man is no more God's image than a hairdresser, nurse's aide or taxicab driver, but the liberals at the seminary failed to realize this. Making them even more offensive is that they were preaching such things in the name of social justice and the kingdom of God! And they would tolerate absolutely no criticism of radical feminism or politically correct dogmas.

They also seemed to believe that being created in the image of God granted certain people a tremendous number of rights without responsibilities. To them, the only responsibility that many people had was to be as politically correct as possible. Other than that, these people may do as they see fit.

As far as I can see it, it does not promote equality when anyone earns 100 times the average per capita income, but most feminists and liberal "social justice" activists would claim that it promotes equality if a woman earned 100 times the average per capita income. In my opinion, such a sentiment places social justice and equality at the service of the rich while neglecting the poor and the working class. [The sentiment that anyone can promote "equality" by earning 100 times the average per capita income is theologically indefensible, and has credibility only when viewed through a cultural lens. I do not believe that Moses, J, E, D, P, or Q had such a view of equality when writing Genesis 1:27. If Feminists were to argue, "Don't you think that ideally women should be guaranteed half of such positions?" I would respond that ideally NO ONE should be earning 100 times the average per capita income until everyone has a sufficiency. Equality does not favor the rich over the poor. I am neither a Marxist nor a communist, but I feel that a sufficiency for all is the highest and most proper form of equality. That being said, I do not condone discrimination on the basis of race or gender at any level, and I feel that all people of all races, genders, and nationalities have the right to a just, equitable, sufficient standard of living. I am neither a politician nor an economist, so I present this as a concept only, and leave it to the experts on how to implement it.]

A highly significant and life-changing dream occurred in October or early November during my second year. I had a dream that I was at another college, and was sitting at a table for lunch when next to me was Danielle, the wonderful and precious girl that I had known from my last months at Genevaville thirteen years earlier. I had hardly even thought about her for the last few years, and when I had the dream many long-buried thoughts from so many years earlier came back.

In this dream, Danielle and I shared a table at a college. She recognized me, though I did not recognize her. She tried to attract my attention. I then introduced myself, and she said, "I know, Jack. I'm Danielle." Since I had the nickname "Jack" for only a short time, I immediately recognized her from a period in the distant past. The dream continued. After the dream, I realized that Danielle was the best friend that I ever had, and that she had changed my life very radically for the better. I knew deep down that I really wanted to marry her, though I sensed that this would be highly unlikely. I thought about what Danielle had in her favor. She was the daughter of a college professor, and scholarships to children of professors was a fringe benefit. I suspected that she performed very highly in college and possibly became a doctor. She was intelligent enough to do so, but I also recalled her severe depression, and feared that she may have committed suicide, though I did not seriously suspect that she had done so. I mailed her a Christmas card, but never got a response, which increased my fear that she may have committed suicide. For the next several weeks after the dream, she was on my mind constantly.

My academic performance was totally respectable. I ended my second year with a 2.97 average, and I would have earned at least 3.0 except that a homiletics professor gave me a C+ grade. Ironically, though I performed worst in my public speaking and homiletics classes than any others (one teacher said that I was his worst student), these were probably the two courses from which I learned the most. Most of the classes were heavily tainted with politically correct propaganda, and the students and faculty could probably tell from my frequent grimaces that I did not agree with or appreciate their one-sided views.

During the second year it was obvious that I would prove unacceptable to most of the faculty, so an agreement was raised where I would be placed in a parish setting for one year. I was assigned to a church in a town that I shall call Egypt.

Most of the parishioners in Egypt were kind to me, but the pastor was not so much satisfied, and informed me several weeks after arriving that I "lacked the social skills" necessary for a clergyman. I had much difficulty in getting along with Mildred, the part-time maid who worked for two days a week. She was very high strung, and easily irritable.

I occasionally visited a church across the river from Egypt. I formed a friendship with Gloria, a very kind and loving woman who attended a charismatic meeting that I occasionally attended, and we have remained friends ever since.

One positive development was that I studied and participated in a Clinical Pastoral Education module at a hospital 45 miles away. The leader, a United

Methodist minister and the four other participants were very kind to me. This turned out to be a positive experience. All five of us students came from homes and childhoods that were dysfunctional to various degrees. One woman was divorced from a Welshman, a very strict Catholic, who had his marriage to her annulled. She was raised Presbyterian, converted to Catholicism, and was highly offended by the annulment, since to her it implied that their marriage was never valid and that their four children were illegitimate. Another woman was a Catholic nun of French-Canadian heritage who was sent to a distant and highly strict French-speaking school for several years, about which she appeared to have negative feelings. The other two participants were a former nun who was raised with an apparently alcoholic father, and a male United Methodist minister.

At our first or second meeting, the instructor gave us a large sheet of paper and asked us to draw some symbol or representation of the view of ministry that each of us had. I drew "SERVICE" in very large letters, and "power" in much smaller letters. I then explained that, to me, being pastoral means service far more than it means power. Many people, and this is true in many churches and denominations as well, have a tremendous lust for power, and such a lust often provided much of the motivation that people have for leadership in church. I saw this lust for power to a nauseous degree at the seminary. I feel that such a lust for power greatly inverts and perverts the real motive for seeking leadership in any church.

Tragically, during a church service in October, I suddenly received unexpected severe flashbacks from enemies at Genevaville and Baggerston Academy many years earlier. These suddenly threw me into a depression and deep fear. It was instantaneous PTSD (post-traumatic stress disorder). I felt totally powerless to suppress this attack. This process accelerated over the next several months, and I became mentally very ill.

Vincent, a friend from Genevaville who arrived there a few weeks before my discharge from there, managed to contact me by mail. I wrote to him regularly, and visited him in his apartment in the slums. He had found a job in a local shoe factory that he held for several years, but was eventually fired from his job and was unemployed thenceforth. Though he tried very hard to study, he had only the equivalent of an eighth grade education at age 18. In January, 1988 I received an unexpected telephone call from the police in his town. The officer said that some letters with my name and address were found in Vincent's apartment, and he informed me that Vincent had suddenly died, and asked for whatever information about Vincent I could share. I was very glad to co-operate, but disappointed that Vincent had died so young. He was only 31 years old. This certainly did not brighten my gloomy, pessimistic outlook on life.

Circa March of that year, I told the members in my clinical pastoral group about my friend Danielle from the distant past, and they told me that I should seek contact with her. Shortly afterward, I worked up the courage to telephone her parents. Her mother answered, and asked who I was and from where I knew Danielle. I suspected that my only hope for happiness was to contact Danielle, form a new friendship with her, and possibly to marry her. Her mother answered, "Danielle is no longer with us." I said, suspecting that she meant suicide, "I was afraid of that." Her mother confirmed my fears about Danielle's suicide, and informed me that she committed suicide in the spring of 1978. I began also to feel a deep sense of guilt, feeling that if I had kept in touch with Danielle over the years I may have been able to have prevented her suicide.

A theory arose among the participants at the Clinical Pastoral Education group as well as with a close friend from the seminary with whom I kept in touch that I was possibly an "adult child of an alcoholic." Several people felt strongly that this was the cause of many if not most of my problems. I inquired to relatives about this, and they informed me that alcoholism and abusive, heavy drinking was prevalent among my male ancestors on every side of the family. Though my father was not technically an alcoholic, he was a heavy problem drinker during his earlier adulthood. His father was such a chronic alcoholic that his doctor gave him an ultimatum that he had to stop drinking or that he would likely die soon. Most of his stomach had to be cut away due to alcohol abuse. My maternal grandmother Nunna, a hard-core temperance teetotaler who I assumed had inherited her rigid Yankee Puritan values from her parents turned out to be the daughter of an alcoholic. And my maternal grandfather was possibly an alcoholic, but his father definitely was an alcoholic and died young as a result. I was told previously that he died from a disease to which bakers were susceptible due to ingredients present in dough, but this turned out to be untrue. The counselor whom I saw at the time also though that the "adult child of an alcoholic" theory may be true, and suggested that I visit Alcoholic Anonymous meetings when I return to Cardiff.

The news of Danielle's suicide made my depression twice as severe as it was before. For the next four weeks or so I got very little sleep. I was even afraid to sleep, for fear of nightmares. This became so severe that I had to be hospitalized at a place 45 miles from Egypt. The night before I had attended a prayer meeting, and one participant said, "I know that you are at the end of your rope."

For the previous several weeks, I had been seeing a counselor approximately 65 miles from Egypt. By now it was obvious that my severe mental illness would make it impossible for me to continue my studies toward ordination. I went to his office for my appointment, and he had planned at my suggestion some questionnaires to help determine a career to which I would be suited. I was so tired from a severe lack of sleep and so unhappy from my severe mental illness that I could not answer any questionnaires or even speak to him for very long. He knew that I needed hospitalization. Fortunately, a hospital 20 to 25 miles away had an opening on its psychiatric unit. It was a relief when I arrived. This greatly stabilized me. I was there for approximately 10 days. Unfortunately, one patient on my wing was a former antagonist from Genevaville, and she immediately recognized me, but she had clearly mellowed. However, I was still relieved when she was discharged.

Another patient on the wing was an Indian (Native American) whose parents were from two different tribes, and was adopted by a white family. I told her that it was likely that I had a small amount of Indian ancestry from my maternal grandmother. Though it has never been proved, it is likely that I have a small amount of Indian ancestry, and I think that anyone who has any Native American ancestry should acknowledge it. Racism against any group should be opposed, and regarded as a major social blight.

CHAPTER SEVEN

On With Adulthood

It had become abundantly obvious that I would not return to the seminary nor continue training for the ministry, so I returned to Cardiff, moved back in with my father in his mobile home, and had immense luck in getting rehired at my old job at the department store. However, my depression remained severe, though not as severe as before the hospitalization, and it made it hard for me to perform at my job, so I was discharged from my job in early November. My boss, however, told me that being kicked out of the ministry was the best thing that ever happened to me. I the meantime, I became suicidal and made at least two half-baked attempts at suicide. I cut my wrist at least once, and I tried drinking some antifreeze. Danielle's parents had told me that she committed suicide by drinking it, but it had no effect on me. My mother told me a few years later that my father was highly worried that he would return home and find me dead from suicide. Around early autumn I lost my suicidal urgings, but remained somewhat depressed for another nine years.

During this time, two of the most popular songs were "Don't Worry, Be Happy" by Bobby McFadden, and "Fast Car" by Tracy Chapman. These songs seemed to be almost directly addressed to me.

I saw various professionals for counseling and various tests. I took a neurological test from a doctor who immensely impressed me with her expertise. She could tell that I had a neurological disorder, but it escaped a diagnosis on the autistic spectrum. I never even heard of autism until several years later.

The "adult child of an alcoholic" theory turned out to be somewhat inaccurate, though heavy alcohol abuse among my ancestors may have contributed to many problems. A few months earlier, I learned that one of my uncles, my mother's brother-in-law, had been an alcoholic since 1973, though he denied it for nearly 15 years. I did attend several Alcoholics Anonymous meetings, but found them somewhat irrelevant since I was not an alcoholic, and very seldom consumed alcohol at all. I am sure, though, that these meetings would be highly helpful to others. They were very helpful to my uncle. I would learn many years later that autism was the real culprit.

During this time I saw an Englishwoman for counseling. She was somewhat helpful, though my negative attitude of hopelessness was so severe that not much could pull me out of it. She tried to convince me that, unlike Danielle and Vincent, I was a survivor.

I was unemployed for only one to two weeks. I quickly found a job at Trapiglione's Pizza in delivery. The "g" is silent of course because in Italian a "g" before an "l" is silent, but I'll call it "Trappi's" for short. At first I did not mind working at Trappi's, and I appreciated a daily source of income due to the tips that I received, but this happy state did not last long. Before much longer, several, if not most, of the employees at Trappi's severely persecuted me for supposedly being gay, and this brought back the trauma from Genevaville earlier. This harassment lasted for at least two years, and greatly declined after the passing of laws against sexual harassment. At least once, someone placed some liquid soap on the door handle of my car to imitate semen, and someone wrote vile epithets in the dust of the rear windshield of my car.

About four weeks after I arrived, a highly prejudiced redneck was hired at Trappi's. He was highly prejudiced against anyone who was different from him in race, religion, or politics and was certainly no credit to the gospel. He was intensely involved in conspiracy theories about the Freemasons, Trilateralists, Bilderbergers, and the other usual suspects. He claimed that secret elitists were building a concentration camp near Bar Harbor, Maine. He intensely hated gays, and was constantly saying hateful things about them. Anytime a new employee arrived, he indoctrinated the newcomer with his hatred of "queers." All in all, he was the most hateful person that I ever knew after leaving Genevaville. I shall call him "Herb."

Several years later, when Herb was hounding a co-worker about the wickedness of "queers," the co-worker said to him, "I don't particularly like queers. But I don't find it necessary to bash queers all the time. If queers leave me alone, I'll leave them alone."

About this time I learned that my good friend Fred from the seminary, though he rarely ever drank alcohol, had concluded that he was an "adult child of an alcoholic," and that this impaired his ability to function as a clergyman. He had decided to delay his ordination, to be placed in a temporary position in a small church to help out the pastor, and soon resigned. He decided that he did not have a vocation. I tried to encourage him that even if his father was an alcoholic, this would not make him any less capable since he did not drink.

As a result of my rapid downward spiral, I quickly lost my faith in God and his love for me. I felt that God had abandoned me, and had not guided my life. I urge all who read this to withhold judgment, as I radically changed my mind nearly one decade later, and now intensely believe in God's love for me and all his human creatures. Nevertheless, I never became an atheist, though my views at the time approached deism, the belief that there was a God who created the world but after that time did little or nothing to intervene in the world or to guide it. I did, however, believe that God's intervention in the life and resurrection of Jesus was an exception to this belief. I must add, with much regret, that most of the highest ranking and most influential theologians and scholars of the "mainline" churches are dedicated to an antisupernatural approach to theology and the Bible that differs little from deism.

In 1991, my mother suggested that I study to be a paralegal. I enrolled at a local junior college. Since I had attended college previously, I was eligible for the one-year certificate program, and did not need to take the two-year associate degree program. I got almost all "A's" in my studies, but it never successfully led to a career.

About this time, my father had a new girlfriend, Debbie. She was divorced, and was previously married to Tracy's uncle. I told her that Tracy was two years behind me in high school, and though I barely knew her, there was a rumor that she had a crush on me, but rejected me when I offered to dance with her. She said, "I wouldn't know anything about that."

Two years after starting at Trappi's a co-worker invited me to visit his Pentecostal church. This was not a typical Pentecostal church, but one which was intensely anti-Trinitarian. It was not Unitarian, like the Unitarian Universalists or the Jehovah's Witnesses, but taught the doctrine of modalism, that the Father, Son and Holy Spirit are all divine but are three modes of one person, rather than three distinct persons. This must be distinguished from the heresy of the Jehovah's Witnesses. I attended for approx. one and one-half years, but never formally joined it. Then I started looking for another church, this one was a Trinitarian Pentecostal church. Circa 1993 I heard of another church which interested me tremendously, though it was at least forty miles from my residence. Due to the distance, I only attended it every four to six weeks. Fortunately, it moved to a location much closer to my home and I started attending far more frequently. It was a "continuing" autonomous branch of an otherwise highly liberal denomination. I found it far more satisfying than either of the two churches that I had attended shortly earlier.

About this time, I began to hear about autism. I never suspected, though, that I had it or that it was the cause of multiple problems for me.

I gradually regained my faith in God and his love. In early 1997, I took a radical leap and decided to give God and faith another try. It worked very happily.

In 1993 my father, brother, and I traveled to France. This was my second trip to France. We arrived at the airport in Paris, and traveled extensively, as far south as Aubagne, near Marseille. We saw some of Normandy as well. My biggest request was to see Normandy, because so many of my ancestors came from there. The French-Canadian side of my family likely came from there, and one English side of my family originally came from there. My great-grandmother's maiden name was Pomroy, and research on the name Pomeroy revealed that our ancestor Ralph de Pomeroy, a Norman conqueror of England in 1066 and close friend of William the Conqueror, came from La Pommeraye (spelled historically several ways) in Normandy. We visited La Pommeraye, and were surprised to find how little was there. There was only one road through this tiny hamlet of fewer than one hundred people, several apple orchards (*La Pommeraye* means *the apple orchard*), one small church and an adjacent cemetery. One villager was rather rude when learning that we were American, and when I told him that I had an ancestor from his village, he did not become any less rude. Nevertheless, it was exciting to visit a place where a historically significant ancestor once called home. We also saw much more of France; indeed we saw more of France than millions of French natives have ever seen of it. My father and I visited France again in 1996. I would later learn that my French-

Canadian ancestors did indeed originally come from Normandy.

In 1997 I encountered a young woman from Vicki's hometown, who had relatives with the same name as Vicki's step-father. She was unfamiliar with Vicki, but tried to track down information about her from relatives. She succeeded in finding a relative who was knowledgeable about her. This woman informed me that Vicki got married, had children, but unfortunately died young. I suspected that she died from the same disease that took her father at a young age. This was truly tragic. I did not learn if Vicki ever succeeded at becoming a nurse, but she was one of the most noble people that I ever knew. I learned many years later that her family was descended from medieval Welsh royalty. I could not help thinking that she was as noble as any of her ancestors could have been.

In the meantime, I became involved with a speakers' group composed of two to four participants with histories of mental illness who gave speeches to patients at hospitals and to professionals who deal with mentally ill clients, and to students preparing for careers in dealing with the mentally ill. This lasted for about three years. At one of our speeches, one of the patients stated, "Suicide is a permanent solution to a temporary problem."

I worked at Trappi's for nearly nine years, and would have found work there far less annoying if it had not been for Herb.

Princess Diana of Great Britain was killed in an auto accident the day before my last day of work at Trappi's, and on my last day I made a delivery to several British women staying at a local hotel. I said to them, "I was sorry to hear about your princess."

The previous Saturday was my first day at my new job: delivering pharmaceuticals.

This was a big step forward, and the co-workers at my new job were far more pleasant and less opinionated than those at Trappi's. The boss was well-known in the community for being charitable and generous, and was a very fine person.

My faith in God as a supernatural, loving being was rapidly returning. However, I remained a very lonely person, and felt that life would not change in this regard. I was by now almost entirely free from my mental illness, but I am not about to stop taking the proper medications. There are still some traces of mental illness and depression.

I placed a bumper sticker on my car saying, "Fish don't walk and Jesus still lives," with an inverted Darwin fish. For some reason, this annoyed my father. When there was a debate over a referendum on gay and lesbian rights, it was reported in the news that a lesbian who had a progay bumper sticker on her car had been antagonized several times on a highway in our state, and I replied, "If she didn't have a lesbian bumper sticker on her car, no one would have known that she was a lesbian and the incident would not have happened." Dad replied, "What if someone doesn't agree with your bumper sticker of 'Jesus saves' and the fish? Do you want them to antagonize you?" I then said, "No, but if they did it would be because I chose to put the bumper sticker on my car. The same with the lesbian."

Things went smoothly in my new job.

In December of 1998, a grocery store approximately 35 miles from my home burned down. It was owned by Tracy's father. In mid-January of 1999, I started to become haunted by flashbacks from the unfortunate incidents involving Tracy and me. It became obsessive and I could not get them out of my mind. Why did several people spread the rumor that Tracy had a crush on me when she did not? Why did Tracy often act as though she had a crush on me? Why did I foolishly let down my guard and give Tracy a chance to reject me? And why did Tracy and her friend put on a big show afterwards to try to convince me that Tracy indeed had a crush on me? This was a time of extreme loneliness in my life, and I had concluded that this would never change.

About this time, though, when I was deeply in prayer I felt God saying, "There's a young woman with a history of mental illness who needs your love."

On the last Thursday of January in 1999, I made a delivery to a group home for disabled adults. A woman in her mid-twenties answered the door. We hit it off very excitedly. This was the most exciting thing that had happened to me for at least twenty years. I knew that I needed to know her better. This excitement made me forget the obsession with Tracy. It was a powerfully healing event.

I did not know, however, if a group home would allow a resident to have a relationship with someone outside the home, but fortunately it was permitted. About three weeks later I called the home and asked for Katherine, and she agreed to go on a date the next Sunday (February 21.) We were both highly excited! I took her to a Chinese restaurant, then we went back to her home. Before I even drove her around the block, she wanted to kiss me! Our first encounter three weeks earlier was love at first sight!

Several days afterward, I remembered the words from my prayers a month earlier, "A young woman with mental illness needs your love!" It indeed came true.

Katherine enriched my life immeasurably. I am highly indebted to her for destroying the immense loneliness in my life.

Katherine was an Asian immigrant adopted by a family in Massachusetts when she was five years old. She told me that she was found on a street and taken to an orphanage. Shortly afterwards, this reminded me of a story I had read in the early 1980s about a Vietnamese girl who was placed in a wooden box but later adopted by an American family. I felt much compassion for Katherine, and felt badly about how tragically her life began and remained.

The biggest trial of my life was about to happen, though I took it very courageously. In late May of 1999, I went to see my doctor for a routine checkup. Suddenly afterward, I felt extreme physical pain, far worse than I ever felt before, while I was still at the clinic. The doctor immediately referred me to the emergency room at a local hospital. The personnel tried to make me a higher priority, though I still ended up waiting for over an hour. My mother met me at the hospital.

The tests confirmed that I had cancer of the kidney. I did not feel frightened or feel sorry for myself, and had no fear of an imminent death. I amazed everyone with my rare courage. Shortly afterwards, Mom drove me back to the clinic, where they gave me a shot that almost immediately killed nearly all the pain.

My mother arranged an emergency appointment at the office of a local urologist. He said that my cancer was almost certain to be malignant. The extreme pain returned, but he did not give me a shot for it, as he felt that the shot would thin my blood to a dangerous level. This decision saved my life.

The doctor arranged for me to have an operation at another local hospital the next Monday; that was the soonest possible. For the next five days, I was in unbelievable pain and had hardly any appetite. I thought that with this experience I now knew how women felt when they gave birth. I did little but to lie in bed. I did have the will to live, but I credit Katherine for giving me the will to live. If it had not been for her, I would not have cared if I lived or died.

The next Monday, my mother drove me to the hospital for the operation. I was thrilled to go! The doctor expected a routine operation that he could perform alone in three hours. Instead, he noticed that in the meantime I had a rupture of my right kidney that caused more than half my blood to clot. I had the biggest blood clot that he had ever seen! Indeed, his earlier decision not to give me a shot for pain had saved my life. Otherwise, a shot probably would have thinned my blood to a very dangerous level. Because of the clot and the rupture, the operation took nine hours, and needed three doctors. In addition, there was considerable damage to my duodenum.

My mother came to visit me in the hospital every night, and my father came several times. A couple from church also came to visit me. I missed Katherine tremendously, though we talked on the telephone frequently. One evening, Mom picked up Katherine and brought her with her. I was in the hospital for 12 days. I was discharged at approximately noon on a Friday. For the first several days after the operation, I was not allowed to eat any solid food, and for the first two days I was not allowed even to drink water but had to melt ice cubes in my mouth. I became very thirsty but not very hungry. I do not understand how I managed not to get hungry. The last two or three days I was served some highly unappetizing food. I lost much weight, but unfortunately it all came back in several weeks.

On the last day in the hospital, my doctor told me that there was a possibility that I might have only two years to live unless my health rebounded. Another cancer patient informed me, though, that such a warning was common practice at the time. I have already lived 16 years since then.

I knew that I had barely missed death. If my doctor were to tell me today that I had only two more years to live, I would accept it graciously and courageously, and thank God for giving me an extra 18 years of life. I knew and know well that my escape from death was very narrow. Without the operation, the blood clot alone would have killed me within one to two days.

For the next two weeks I could not go to work, nor was I allowed to drive a car. For the four weeks after that, I was allowed to work three to four hours a day, and to drive a car on a limited basis.

And, give God and my employer the glory and thanks, only briefly before I was diagnosed with the disease my employer had promoted me to a full time status, which made me eligible for health coverage, which at the time was an HMO (health maintenance organization policy.) Had it not been so, my previous and highly limited coverage would have proved highly insufficient, and I would have had tens of thousands of dollars in debt. God was watching over me!

Katherine and I had wonderful times together. In late summer of 1999 we traveled to Prince Edward Island, Canada, and we loved it. She certainly has had more than her share of ups and downs, especially downs.

Sadly, we had a major disagreement in June of 2001, and she broke up with me. I was very, very saddened by this, and was even abusive to some innocent people because of this. During this time, four proof silver eagles ($1.00 silver bullion coins) arrived. Ordinarily this would have excited me, but they did nothing to make me happier. They were futile in helping me forget the tremendous loss in my life. I begged Katherine to get back together with me. A couple days later, she relented and agreed. We had many happy times that summer.

Later that summer, my mother and I went to a family reunion in Cardiff at a local church. The wife of a distant relative traced our ancestry to a village near Dieppe in Normandy, France, to an ancestor who settled in Ste-Famille on the Isle d'Or leans in Quebec, Canada. In October, Katherine and I visited Ste-Famille. We found a church with small cemeteries on either side, where some ancestors and distant relatives were buried. Also, to my delight, we found a three-sided stone which contained the names of three pioneer brothers, one of whom was my direct ancestor. We also stopped in Quebec City, where we saw the Hotel Frontenac (no trip to Quebec City would be complete otherwise) and the Montmorency Falls.

I had recently moved out of my father's mobile home and into an apartment across from where I worked. This sure was convenient! My father was very disappointed that I moved out.

The next three years were rather uneventful, but in May of 2005 my father died from a sudden stroke. Shortly afterwards, I moved back to his mobile home, where I lived until September of 2010.

At this time, my brother and mother were involved in a scheme to deprive me of my control of the money that I had inherited from my father. They had a local attorney draw up a document to set up a "trust fund," which would put total control of my inheritance in the hands of my mother and later my brother. This would require my signature since my father in no way required that my inheritance be placed into such a fund. My mother had no confidence in my ability to handle such a large sum of money. As the document was originally written, I had no right to make withdrawals from the fund, and this would remain in force until my death. That meant that I would be subject to the whims of Mom and Sam to the money that was rightfully mine, even after age 65. I initially refused to approve this proposed document. Shortly afterward, the attorney met with my mother and me, and I voiced my objection. He suggested that the proposal could be amended, to allow me to withdraw per year the greater of $5,000.00 or 5% of the value of the trust fund without the permission of Mom or Sam, and that I would gain total control of the Trust Fund at age 65. With these improvements, I agreed. In the attorney's presence, Mom agreed to grant me a lump sum of $10,000. I should have had a document drafted and had her sign it in the attorney's presence, since she later reneged on her word. The attorney also said that the document was irrevocable, meaning that no party or any future attorney could recall or revoke its terms. (Five years later, another attorney did exactly that.)

A few months afterwards, my mother developed breast cancer and one of her breasts needed to be surgically removed.

The following is highly significant. In September of 2007, Katherine's brother in North Carolina got married, and Katherine and I were invited. Katherine's parents also treated us to one week at a rented home on the Outer Banks in Corolla, North Carolina. There I met many of Katherine's relatives, including her aunt Anne. Providentially and fortunately for me, Anne was a neurological nurse practitioner. When I was not present, Anne told Katherine and other relatives that I likely had some degree of autism. Katherine told me of this three weeks later, and suggested that I seek professional counseling.

Shortly afterwards, back in Cardiff, I started meeting with a counselor, Abe. I discussed with him the theory that I had some degree of autism. I also discussed it with my mother, who had an associate degree in psychology, though it never led to a career, and had read substantially. She thought that I might have been autistic as well.

In earlier years, the word *yuppie* was highly in vogue. My brother had become a big-achieving yuppie in Texas, and even Mom had called him a yuppie. However, about this time, my mother developed an intense hatred of this word, and reacted very angrily when I persisted in using it, whether in reference to Sam or anyone else. Additionally, when I once used this word in the presence of some of Katherine's relatives, Katherine told me a couple of weeks later that her relatives found my use of this world to be mildly, but not egregiously, ignorant and offensive. My mother threw such a fit whenever I said "yuppie" in her presence that I no longer dared to use it around her.

Mom had "connections" at a local university. She had a friend who was a retired dean there, who arranged for me to have a neuro-psychological evaluation with a supervised graduate student. This student gave me a sufficient battery of relevant tests. This confirmed that I had Asperger's Syndrome, which is not a severe form of autism but is on the autistic spectrum. I am indebted to all those who helped me toward getting this diagnosis. Sometimes Asperger's Syndrome is called "high-functioning autism," a term which is used inconsistently.

This settled many, many questions about the origins of my multiple problems. For many years, my mother though that my disorders may have been caused because I was born while my mother was under anesthetics, but this was discredited by a neurological exam in 1988. Unfortunately, this exam failed to detect Asperger's Syndrome or any other degree of autism, though it did confirm a neurological disorder.

It is remarkable that denominations that appeal chiefly to the upper-middle and upper classes are the ones that are most rapidly declining in membership, while the denominations that appeal chiefly to the working classes are either growing, holding their own, or declining only slowly. The more conservative churches have far more appeal to the working classes than the so-called mainline churches. And while the mainline churches brag so much about their commitment to "diversity," the more conservative churches tend to be far more diverse in their membership, and have far more appeal to the working classes, minorities, and immigrants. The leaders of the more conservative and evangelical churches are far more likely to treat lower-class and working-class people as equals, while many in the mainline churches often see these people as tools to be manipulated for political purposes. Indeed, multitudes of mainline church leaders denounce movements and clergy that appeal chiefly to the less wealthy as "anti-intellectual." Liberals do so to assert their alleged superiority; they are not very humble. In this regard, conservative and evangelical churches are far more egalitarian than the mainline churches. Incidentally, when Jesus said that no one can enter the kingdom of God without approaching it as a little child, he was not being anti-intellectual. With my IQ of 132-136, I sure hope that he was not. But he was teaching that all people, including intellectuals, should be humble.

Additionally, if not ironically, the more conservative churches emphasize doctrines that are far more egalitarian. The doctrine that all human beings are sinners treats everyone equally and discriminates against no one. The doctrine that Jesus died for all and that salvation through faith in Christ is available to all people of all classes and abilities is highly egalitarian. As an autistic person, I consider this highly important. Many liberal mainliners, on the other hand, consider upper-class gender quotas, political correctness, and the promotion of antimale sentiment and retribution to be more important. I consider such to be a preferential option for the rich. Classism seems to be common within the mainline liberal churches, but rare among conservative churches.

Back to my autism. When I got the diagnosis for Asperger's Syndrome, I was inclined toward self-pity for a very short period of time. Why did I have to be the unlucky one in 180 people of my generation to get autism? But the diagnosis and understanding that I was on the autistic spectrum proved to be highly liberating. I realized that I was not so unintelligent as I had long thought. (I figured that I had faked by in high school to get such high grades.) I now feel that I am better off and more successful than 97% of people with autism. However, that still does not pay all the bills. The "glass ceiling" for autistic individuals is very low.

In early April of 2010, my mother's health took a sudden turn for the worse. The breast cancer that she had 4 ½ years earlier had metastasized. It spread to the back of her shoulder. None of us, though, anticipated an imminent death.

In the spring of 2010, I decided to study at a local on-line school for a *semi*-professional career that would take approximately two years to learn. I excelled at it, and finished studies in the spring of 2012. I did an "externship," (a term for an internship in such a field of study) at a location approximately 45 miles from my home. I did not get this promotion, though, for several months. I think that someone in a position of influence who has an autistic relative and knew that I was autistic helped me get it, plus the former owner (who probably knew of my autism) was also helpful.

In late May, I got a call from my uncle (Mom's brother-in-law) that Mom had been suddenly hospitalized, but that she was all right. A visit to her at the hospital revealed that she had only several months to live. This took most of us by surprise. She was only 75. She was a strong health enthusiast. She was very thin and substantially underweight, and ate very little besides fruits, vegetables and fish. We had long assumed that she would live until her late eighties at least. Sam even said that he and I might die before Mom. This hit us all like a ton of bricks. At least we had a warning of Mom's approaching death; it would not hit us off-guard or unexpectedly. My brother took it far harder than I did, but neither of us was at all happy.

On the first Saturday of her hospital stay, Mom hired a lawyer to draft her final will, who was willing to meet her in her hospital room. I attended, in hopes of coaxing Mom not to disfavor me. Mom assured me that she would grant me a lump sum of $15,000.00 and put the remainder in the trust fund. This was agreeable to me, but once again Mom reneged on her word. She put all my portion into the trust fund, where I would have no access to it. To add insult to injury, Mom's attorney charged $5,000.00 to merge the trust funds, paid out of my trust fund.

Shortly afterward, I was notified that not only had Mom's attorney allowed Mom to go back on her word, but that she also merged my trust fund of 2005 with this new trust fund of 2010, and that my rights to remove the greater of $5,000.00 or 5% a year were revoked. I was very angry at my mother for cheating me as such. She had been resentful of my legal right to withdraw money from the previous trust fund without her approval.

For many decades, I felt that my mother favored my brother Sam to me. On several occasions I let her know about my feelings about this, and she would respond, "I don't know why you'd feel that way," or "I put up with you all these years," but she never once directly or explicitly denied that she favored Sam over me.

I feel that political disagreements between my mother and me were part of her motivation for disfavoring me, and that her unfair treatment of me was revenge on her part. My brother was so wealthy that she had no chance of controlling him, but she knew that she could control me, even after her death. It was a vengeful feminist's dream come true.

For the next three or four weeks, I got only about four hours of sleep each night. It is a wonder that I could have functioned at my job during that period.

My brother, who has lived in Texas since the early 1990s, came to Cardiff and stayed for two to three weeks, but had no choice but to travel to Russia on business. While he was in Russia, he was informed that Mom had died. He shortly notified me by cell phone.

I wrote the eulogy for my mother at her funeral, which Sam was unable to attend. Following is the eulogy:

"It us both easy and hard to write a eulogy about my mother.

As many of you know, in the mid-1950s my mother was a [professional ballerina.] She was an outstanding dancer and ballerina. But I feel quite confident that her proudest achievement is her two sons, my brother [Sam] and I.

Due to a significant disability that I have had all my life, I was a difficult and challenging child to raise, and this gave her tremendous grief for many years. But she never gave up on me.

Many of my happiest memories of our times together involved traveling to the coast each summer…We also traveled to Boston and New York City, where she showed me where she once performed.

My mother was a person of "tough love," who seldom gave me my way or grant my desires but it paid off for me in the long run.

She tried many times to make me happy, such as [during] long school vacations which could become boring. She arranged for me to get the medical and other care that I needed. Through the ups and downs for decades she was there for me. I was sick for much of the first three years of elementary school, but she took very good care of me.

In late October of 1971, she and my father separated. The next day was a very sad day for by brother and me. We were worried if we would get to see our father again, and begged Mom to reconcile with Dad. Fortunately, they were separated for only one day. Many years later I gave my mother a silver medallion with the date 10-30-71 engraved on it to thank my mother for being reconciled to my father for the welfare of her children.

Once she brought home a turkey pie from [a local bakery.] At first it did not look very appetizing or attractive, but after I tried it I loved it! It was a very pleasant surprise.

Over the past three years my mother and I learned the true cause of my condition: I have been diagnosed with Asperger's Syndrome, a form of partial autism. Things then changed rapidly, and I became convinced that I was indeed a successful person for having overcome such formidable barriers. But my mother knew all along that I was successful. I have had a full-time job for over eleven years, and am training to become a deacon at my church. I am now studying at [a local technical school] and have scored very high on my tests. God obviously knew that he could entrust to my mother a child with special needs, and I believe that God is very pleased with how she raised me."

After Mom died, Sam came up with a truly brilliant idea. We inherited a large building in downtown Cardiff with two business units and one very large apartment, where my mother had lived for her final years. Sam suggested that I move there, sell my mobile home, and he would allow me to rent that apartment for $500.00 per month, which would be my payment for his share of ownership. This would work to the benefit of both of us. A comparable apartment would cost $1,000.00 to $1,500.00 per month otherwise. Unfortunately, it took seven months to sell my mobile home, which forced me to waste thousands of dollars in lot rental, heating expenses, expenses for shoveling, and property taxes.

I learned in 2018 that my mother's promising career as a ballerina in the mid-1950's was ended because her colleagues informed her that in order to advance, she would need to provide sexual favors to a certain powerful man in the industry. My earlier book criticized many fallacies and inadequacies of Political Correctness and Radical Feminism. But on this issue, I'm with the Feminists 90%. The other 10% is because Feminists would condemn men collectively, en masse, for such depravities and some have said that if innocent men suffer from false charges, such is justified because at least it will weaken "patriarchy." But *no woman from any social class, or in any occupation, should have to submit to such depraved demands* in order to get a job or to further her career. This tragic occurrence may easily explain why my mother was so negative toward heterosexual men and seemed unable to form friendships with such men though she had some close gay male friends.

CHAPTER EIGHT

Reflections On My Life

Now that I look back on my life I realize that things are, and much of the time were, much better than I thought and that positive things occurred that I did not allow to sink deeply into my thoughts. I feel that I am more successful than 97% of people on the autistic spectrum and among people with a history of mental illness. When the Englishwoman that I saw for counseling told me that, unlike Danielle and Vincent I was a survivor, I immediately thought, "Big deal! At least they are out of their misery, while I have years if not decades of depression ahead of me." I realize that decades of self-pity were counter-productive to an extreme degree. I realized decades too late that Tracy had a good reason for rejecting me; for the first three weeks of the school year she was highly cordial and enthusiastic toward me while I was cynical and somewhat rude toward her. I changed my attitude toward her early in the fourth week, but it was too little and too late. She lost interest in me.

As an autistic person I am constantly reminded about how I was and am different from most others. Other people get excited about many foods that they enjoy while I find most of them highly unpleasant.

The multitude of social problems caused by autism made me unmarriageable. When I hear others talk enthusiastically about their children, it sometimes makes me aware about how I never had children. I try to comfort myself that because I do not have any children I had more time and money for myself and my hobby of numismatics and will never need to pay the impossible and ridiculously high prices of college tuition for children. At the same time I realize that if I had children, there is a high likelihood that one or all of them might be autistic, especially since the science of finding the causes of autism is still in its infancy. It does occasionally make me sad when Katherine and I go to beaches and swimming pools and see delightful young children and realize that I will never have any. I comfort myself in realizing that I will never have to worry about having children who may become drug addicts or criminals. Nevertheless, I am constantly reminded that I turned out differently from most people due to autism. None of this, however, means that others should be deprived of the pleasure and pride of children due to a need to be "sensitive" to childless individuals. I hope that the time never comes when political correctness demands that people not speak of their children on the grounds that speaking of one's children makes a person "insensitive" to childless individuals. People should love and be proud of their children, even if not all of them grow up to become lawyers or doctors.

There is insecurity in not knowing if others know about my autism or if my appearance and mannerisms give me away as being "different." Undoubtedly dozens of people have falsely thought that I was gay because of such differences and because I did not fit the "mold." Though I do not regard political correctness and feminism as absolutely perfect sacrosanct movements, I agree wholeheartedly with feminists that women (and for that sake anyone) should not need to tolerate sexual harassment. I, though male and heterosexual, have suffered immeasurably from sexual harassment, and feel that no one should be subjected to such abuse. After badly needed laws against sexual harassment were passed in the early 1990s, such harassment against me at work subsided greatly.

Life for me has improved greatly and nearly steadily since I regained my faith in God and his love since 1997. My mental illness has nearly disappeared, and my faith has become very strong. That small church that I have attended regularly since circa 1994 has been a tremendous blessing to me, and I have been recently ordained as a deacon. Just before ordination I realized that my responsibilities before my congregation, God, and humanity itself would greatly increase, but I am aware of 2 Corinthians, "My grace is sufficient for you, for in grace weakness reaches perfection." And, unlike many people who so arrogantly feel that they and they alone have the proper understanding of grace, I feel that God's grace should make everyone who receives it very humble. If this grace does not make us humble, then we have a highly corrupt understanding of grace; there is never anything wrong with God's grace. Some people who preach the loudest about "pure grace," "grace alone," etc., are anything but humble. They need far more humility. And the rest of us do as well.

My job has brought me into contact with dozens of people with neural (nerve-related), intellectual, psychological, and emotional disabilities. Katherine has been a tremendous blessing to me, and has done what no one else ever accomplished: destroying the loneliness in my life. I have seen many, many people who are mentally ill or have autism or Down's syndrome or other disabilities.

For many years I often thought, though I never made a vow to God about it, that if I could know another woman like Danielle, I would be willing to give up my coin collection for her. Obviously I did not carry through with this. This coin collection had caused immense conflicts with Katherine and my mother. It is highly likely that one major reason why my mother schemed to prevent me from control of my inheritance is that she was afraid that I would "go off the deep end" by spending tens of thousands of dollars on rare coins.

I drive a humble though dependable and adequate car. I would not buy any "yuppie" luxury car. Since 2007 I have supported a girl in Uganda, though she tragically died from cerebral malaria in the late spring of 2015.

In 2007 I admitted to Katherine that over the previous two years since my father's death, I had spent over $3,000.00 on coins. Katherine quickly became angry at me, saying, "You spent thousands of dollars on coins while you say that you can't afford my groceries." I term myself a recovering numismaholic. You will not find this strange word in any dictionary. I coined (no pun intended) that word. It means a person chronically addicted to acquiring and collecting coins. It can be as much of an addiction as drugs or alcohol, and represented a failure on my part. It has taken many years to break from this addiction. Shortly before my mother died, I said to her, "I don't own my coin collection. My coin collection owns me." Recently I have sold many coins, at big losses, to pay my bills. There are multitudes of dishonest and unscrupulous individuals who sell overgraded coins at highly inflated prices. The advent of "slabbing" in the mid-1980s sought to reduce the widespread abuses in the numismatic market, but this was only a partial and temporary success. While there is still at least one highly reputable slabbing service, there are several not so reputable services, and some which were once reliable are now far less reliable than they once were. All of this has caused me to become highly disillusioned with numismatics. This disillusionment, however, is a blessing in disguise as it has helped me curb my greed for coins, which greed (like most forms of greed) made me less sensitive to the needs of others. I must blame my own tendency to greed for the problems that being a numismaholic has caused me.

I firmly believe that the world needs Jesus and the full, complete gospel more than anything, and that these can change the world immeasurably. Unfortunately, virtually all denominations, churches, and sects have failed miserably, including the evangelicals and fundamentalists who so self-righteously claim to be "perfectly biblical" in doctrine and practice, and are very quick to condemn all other denominations. No one is consistently biblical in practice unless they love their neighbors as themselves.

I believe that one of the greatest failures of Christians of all denominations is their failure to speak out about the wickedness of greed. Evangelicals widely quote Romans 1 to attack the active practice of homosexuality. But they rarely quote the rest of the chapter, which condemns "covetousness" or "greed" (depending on the translation) as a form of wickedness that deserves death. I am not, of course, promoting capital punishment for greedy people; God will judge them as he sees fit. But when the Bible condemns greed as a wickedness that deserves death, I feel that we must take seriously that greed is indeed sinful and wicked. Christ also condemned greed as a wicked design that originates in the human heart, along with other sins. (Mark 7:17-23) In doing so, he was denying that greed (and other sins) originate in or exist only in "social structures," contradicting what many modern liberal theologians teach.

I am very disappointed that liberal so-called Christian social justice activists have failed miserably to take a firm, consistent stand against greed. If they are so zealous for the kingdom of God (which many of them equate with earthly human justice and progress) then they need to take a courageous and clear stand against greed, since Ephesians 5:5 condemns greed as a form of idolatry that will keep its practitioners out of the kingdom of Christ and God. Instead, they wish to be fashionable with the secular humanist elite and politically correct cultural elites by blaming "sexism" for nearly all of America's problems. They should be condemning greed at least five times for every time they condemn "sexism." But that will not sit well with the cultural elites. Again, they should ram Ephesians 5:5 instead of the highly misleading, invalid, and fallacious "76 cent" figure down people's throats.

Before I can be America's preacher of anti-greed, I must overcome my own greed. And God's grace is sufficient for this!

Recently I have realized that if we want God to bless our dreams and to make them a reality, then we must dream in accord with God's word. Since his word so severely condemns greed (and rightly so), if we dream greedy dreams, then we are dreaming in conflict with his word. We should not complain or lose faith when he does not bless our sinful desires. God's severe condemnation of greed is not an obstacle to the fulfillment or happiness of individuals, but is an act of his extreme love for humanity. Feminists are quick to assert that "sexism" oppresses the female half of humankind, but the greed of the wealthy oppresses the overwhelming majority. To put it otherwise, the greed of the top 1% (one percent) oppresses 70% to 99% of the population.

Greed is a way of saying, "I love my luxuries, my mansions, my fleet of luxury cars, my gold, my silver, and my other superfluous possessions more than I love my neighbor." Jesus ordered his followers to love their neighbors as themselves, and Paul wrote that whoever loves one's neighbor has fulfilled the law. (Romans 13:9-10). I fully accept the teaching that we are justified by grace alone, but I do not feel that God's grace was ever intended to be a license for disobedience to Jesus, God, or his word.

I do not blame God for humanity's problems. In his word and through his son Jesus, the prophets, and the apostles, God did intervene in teaching us how to live and taught us to love God and our neighbor. If we accepted biblical teachings about greed and love of neighbor, our social problems would decline immensely. When atheists and other unbelievers complain that God does not intervene to prevent problems, I respond by saying, "Yes, he did intervene. But we decided to ignore his instructions."

Having made new friends and acquaintances over the years, and having had more contact with numerous others and becoming more sensitive to others and their trials and sufferings instead of being pre-occupied with my own, I now feel sorry for myself far less. One unfortunate tendency of autistic and mentally ill persons is to be pre-occupied with their own problems and miseries, and I was that way for many years. As a requirement for ordination I needed to receive a psychological evaluation. I went to a professional, Dr. Dubois, whom I knew from Genevaville more than forty years earlier for such an evaluation. His report stated that I had overcome by 35% (thirty-five percent) the effects of Asperger's Syndrome since my evaluation in late 2009.

I have tried, with God's help of course, to evaluate my life in accord with Holy Scripture and to orient my values with those of scripture. Colossians 1 informs us that all things were created through Christ and for him. Thus, we were not created for our own self-fulfillment but for the glory of Christ. I also realized that I must remove all greed and covetousness from my life.

Tragically, nearly all denominations are, in my opinion, depriving both their own members and humanity by emphasizing a small number of fewer than two dozen proof texts and ignoring nearly all the rest of scripture. I am in agreement with evangelicals and fundamentalists that eternal salvation is priority number one for Christian believers. However, so much of the Bible, including the New Testament, speaks so much about personal virtue, love of neighbor, rejection of personal sins such as greed, and justice which I feel includes social justice as well.

Many evangelicals and fundamentalists seem to feel that correctness on the doctrine of justification is of such extreme importance that little else matters. As I recently said, they are correct to be concerned about salvation and justification, and are correct that these come from God's grace alone and must be received in faith. But there is so much else to the gospel and the New Testament! Most people today, unless they are highly dedicated Christians, regard salvation as irrelevant at best, and *these people are wrong!*

Jesus asked why people call him Lord but do not do as he says. (Luke 6:46) He also challenged people to let their light shine before [others] so that they may see goodness in your acts and give glory to the heavenly Father. (Matthew 5:16) Any concern for obedience and good works makes millions of evangelicals and fundamentalists suspicious of "works righteousness" and denials of "faith and grace alone." I allege that it is possible to believe in faith and grace alone without being indifferent to obedience to God and being charitable at the same time. The Gospels all pre-suppose such. They are full of commands to charity, love of neighbor, and concern for justice without denying or contradicting faith and grace alone. Much of this is found in Paul's letters as well. I do not believe that grace alone and faith alone were even intended to be a license to sin, or to disobedience. While many theological liberals reduce the virtues and faith of scripture and Christianity to socialism, Marxism, and radical feminism, their evangelical counterparts often reduce love of neighbor and other virtues to a mere desire to convert people to evangelical Protestantism while ignoring charity, justice, and many other virtues. This is one big reason why we as Christians are losing the battle for souls.

It is true that our Savior once said that two of you on earth agree on one thing, it shall be granted by their Father in heaven. (Matthew 18:19) This verse has been misused and abused greatly by "prosperity" preachers whose message is that if a working-class Christian desires an extravagant yuppie luxury car of a certain color, it shall be granted by God. (But only if such a person tithes to the prosperity preacher!) Do not be misled! When anyone prays for anything, they should never pray for anything contrary to the word of God! They should not pray for greedy dreams, because greed is contrary to God's will. Yes, God allows some people to become wealthy yuppies. But these people, and everyone else, should not be greedy.

It is also true that Jesus once said he came that they may have life to the fullest. (John 10:10) This text has also been misused and abused by those on both the left and the right. Many people, if not most, have dreams for greed and power and other lusts that come at the expense of others. To claim that God would fulfill any selfish dream implies that God loves such a selfish person's dreams while being unconcerned about those who are victimized by such. Since Jesus taught self-denial rather than self-fulfillment, he could not have been teaching self-fulfillment in this verse. Jesus said that it is in losing one's life that one finds one's life. He was teaching fulfillment, but not self-fulfillment. He taught that one finds one's true fulfillment, which requires service to Christ, through faith and virtues. One finds true fulfillment through serving and being a blessing to others, rather than in gaining as much money, prestige, and luxuries for oneself as possible. Since we were created for Christ (Colossians 1), we find our only true reason for existence through faith in him and serving him. If we are living only for our own *self-fulfillment*, we have defeated our purpose for living, contrary to what our surrounding culture tells us.

All of this has been of tremendous benefit to me as an autistic, working-class Christian. Yes, in the past I have had many greedy dreams, fueled by my numismatic addiction. It was about self-fulfillment, not true fulfillment. The message that we get from our surrounding culture is that fulfillment comes only from having a high-paying, powerful career that bestows much prestige, and that the more money we earn the more of a success we are. This, I feel, severely attacks the self-esteem of the vast majority of the population. I documented in my earlier book that less than 2% (two percent) of men in the United States were doctors or lawyers, along with the assertion that at most 4% (four percent) of the populace could have the high-paying prestigious careers that so many people consider necessary for "success." The news media, the entertainment media, the feminists, and sometimes even the mainline churches (and to be fair, the prosperity preachers) are thus making success and self-esteem impossible for the vast majority of both women and men.

It is of great importance that all Christians, both the clergy and the laity, should read the Bible, at least the New Testament, eagerly and zealously. In the Bible one will learn that it is God's will for people to be generous, free from greed and other forms of wickedness, loving toward one's neighbor, humble, grateful to Jesus for his teachings and atonement on the cross for our sins, and many other virtues. One cannot necessarily learn from the Bible if it is God's will for a particular person to become a foreign missionary or what job or career to enter, but one can easily learn the importance of grace, faith, love, and virtues, which are God's will for all people. WE NEED YOU, JESUS!

My coin collection made me insatiably greedy. I therefore, though merely a working-class person, know what greed is like and its destructive power. No matter what rare, beautiful coins I had purchased, I always wanted more and more and I could not buy enough of them to be satisfied with life. Such scriptures as Ephesians 5:5 (condemning greed as a sin which would keep people out of the kingdom of Christ and God) and 1 Timothy 6:6-10 (which teaches contentment with a sufficiency) were very helpful. I analyzed my life in the light of these passages, and saw my spiritual failures. These two passages alone could do much to transform the world, not to mention the thousands of other biblical passages.

It has been said that the opposite of love is not hatred but indifference. I cannot find any exact parallel to that in scripture, but Jesus' command to love our neighbor as ourselves rules out both hatred and indifference.

One reason why I feel that it of great importance that Christians, both laity and clergy, should read the Bible for themselves is because it contains so much that few on either the left or the right dare to preach. Few on either side dare to take a strong, consistent, and counter-cultural stand against greed, and millions are pre-occupied with their favorite dozen to two dozen proof texts while ignoring so much of the Bible. This includes evangelicals, many of whom smugly regard themselves as the only biblically faithful Christians. We also need to develop the biblical virtues, though relatively few dares to preach about the need for them, partly because they fear that evangelicals will accuse them of promoting "works righteousness" and denying "grace alone." *We need a balance in applying biblical themes!* And we need to be *humble* about receiving God's grace and not be presumptuous about it!

Evangelicals are not all bad! I give them credit for defending and upholding such doctrinal essentials as the virgin birth, universal human sinfulness, God's nature as a supernatural being, the atonement of Christ for human sin, the Trinity, as well as the Incarnation of the second person of the Trinity as Jesus Christ, while many liberals junk these essentials as anti-intellectual myths disproved by modern philosophy. Augustine and Thomas Aquinas were intellectual giants, there was nothing anti-intellectual about them, and they wholeheartedly believed in the biblical truths of historic Christianity.

We also need a more consistent application of Christian, biblical themes to our many national and international woes. Jesus taught us to forgive those who wronged us, and Paul taught us to reject all bitterness (Ephesians 4:31). This command to forgive is even reflected in the Lord's Prayer.

Humility promotes true equality. Many upscale individuals who regard themselves as the most egalitarian people alive would never dream of treating mechanics, electricians, construction workers, let alone nurse's aides or waitresses as their equals. Scriptures tells us to have the same mind toward all, not to mind high things, and to associate with those of low estate. (Romans 12:16) A billionaire is no more God's image than a nurse's aide or waiter. That is the "flip" side of equality.

The need is great for a truly Christian sub-culture which prizes humility, family, service, faith, self-denial, and which gets its motivation from love of neighbor rather than love of money, wealth, power, and luxury. It should, however, engage and challenge the dominant cultural values of Hollywood, the news media, and other major institutions rather than withdraw from the wider culture. We need a cultural revolution from the bottom up, rather than from the top down.

According to Colossians 1:16, all things were created through Christ and for him. That is why each of us is here: to be the servants of Christ. That is how we fulfill our purpose for existence. The Biblical Virtues, as I call them, are the path to peace and true fulfillment. They do not reflect the values of our surrounding culture, or probably any other culture. Romans 12:2 tells us not to be conformed to this world, but to be transformed by the renewing of our minds. We are to resist the sinful pull of the world, and to be a positive influence through our faith and virtues.

Hebrews 11:6 informs us that it is impossible to please God without FAITH. While many see this as "discrimination" against atheists and other non-believers and unbelievers, I see it instead as a qualification. It is not discrimination to deny admittance to a medical graduate school to an applicant who does not meet the qualifications of an undergraduate degree. Likewise, it is not discrimination to deny the benefits of faith to those who lack it. Justice is whatever God declares it to be, and he has declared that we are justified by FAITH.

Currently I am going through a very difficult time economically. I must have faith, whether it is easy or not, that God will lead me out of it. God allowed this to happen to cleanse me from greed. I have needed to sell nearly all my coins to pay off debts. I have received some benefit from this. My coin collection promoted greed, which led to indifference to my neighbors. Jesus was indeed correct when he said that no one can serve both God and Mammon (money or wealth as an idol.) Ephesians 5:5 teaches that greed (or covetousness) is idolatry. I have since learned that my coins were a "security blanket" and that I do not need them as a false source of security. I have been strengthened in realizing this.

Hebrews 12:5-8 tells us that God disciplines us as a father disciplines his children, and that if we reject such discipline, we are not his children but are bastards.

As to the charge that faith in God and Christ are "discriminatory" against unbelievers, I shall respond by saying that there are certain egalitarian elements in Christian faith that exist nowhere else. Through

Christ, people of all social strata and abilities and disabilities may enter God's Kingdom unto eternal glory. Each of us can serve Christ. As an autistic person whose earthly potential was limited, this means a great deal to me. We hear from secular sources and some liberal theologians about the glories of self-fulfillment and "self-actualization" but what about people who do not have much earthly potential to fulfill? What about the vast majority of women and men who do not have the potential to acquire upscale careers, for reasons totally unrelated to "discrimination?" Many of these people have more economic need than those who have acquired upscale careers. I feel that our cultural elites have failed such people. But people of all social strata have the ability, through faith, to enter God's eternal Kingdom.

The Bible has much to say about this, though most "social justice" activists overlook most of it. Jesus taught that many of the last shall come first and many of the first shall come last; such is the dynamic of God's Kingdom. James 2:4-6 tells us that the poor have been chosen by God to be rich in faith, and condemns discrimination against the poor, which can often be very subtle.

Does the Bible teach equality? To be sure. But our cultural elites' understanding of equality is not necessarily God's definition of it. I feel that the strongest statement for social justice and equality is 1 Timothy 6:6-10:

But godliness with contentment is great gain: for we brought nothing into the world, for neither can we carry anything out; but having food and covering we shall be therewith content. But they that are minded to be rich fall into a temptation and a snare and many foolish and hurtful lusts, such as drown men in destruction and perdition. For the love of money is a root of all kinds of evil: which some reaching after have been led astray from the faith, and have pierced themselves through with many sorrows. (American Standard Version)

I would not take this 100% literally; obviously we need more than food and clothing. But the deep meaning of this verse is to be content with a sufficiency, and not to be greedy.

This passage takes a stronger stand for social justice and equality in five verses than nearly anyone ever said in volumes. I fondly call it "The Magna Carta of Social Justice and Equality." Because we are all equally the Image of God no one has any God-given rights from such that others do not have. It does not give anyone the right to be fabulously wealthy, as the wealthy are no more God's image than the poor; the "flip side" of equality. There are legitimate reasons for inequalities in wealth and income such as more experience, responsibilities, skills, education, and expertise, but being created in the Image of God is not among them.

I thank God for having survived cancer for nineteen years, along with my mostly good health, and that both of my parents lived until I was well into my adult years, along with my healing from mental illness.

Jesus informed us in Matthew 23:12 that those who exalt themselves shall be humbled, and that those who humble themselves shall be exalted. It shall happen to all of us sooner or later, so let us humble ourselves now!

The Bible so frequently teaches how God exalts the lowly, and coaxes all toward humility. The Gospel, though it is concerned about eternal life and glory (e.g. John 3:16) is profoundly social. This does NOT mean that it can be reduced to any political party or system, and no one can gain salvation through any kind of political activism. Because God loved us first, and granted his totally undeserved gift of grace to us, we should respond to his commands, especially to be compassionate and forgiving, generous and loving. God's grace is prevenient, meaning that it "comes before," before any response on our part, and grace is not earned. These lessons from the Bible about personal virtue, that Christ died for me and all other sinners, that God's grace came before my response or anyone else's, have helped me greatly to realize the true purpose of life. It has made an otherwise unbearable life indeed bearable, to help me see my blessings, to analyze my failures in the light of Scripture, and to allow God to correct such failures.

My life has value before God despite nearly all earthly lack of success. So can anyone else's life. God has purged me from my greed, so that I will be less indifferent to those in need. God has made me more sensitive to others. He has given me extraordinary critical analytical thinking skills not for my glory but for the service of others. It is in serving Christ that one can find one's true purpose in life, and through submission to the counsels of Scripture toward virtue, along with a much-tested faith, that I find true meaning in life. These, along with knowing about the glorious eternal heavenly Kingdom that Jesus gained for those of his faith make life worth living.

For a deeper understanding of the biblical virtues, I recommend my earlier book, *Toward a Balanced Message,* especially Chapter 6, "The Social Code of the Bible."

Praise to our Lord and Savior, Jesus Christ! AMEN!

UPDATE TO THE REVISION OF 2023

Since writing the main body of this autobiography five years ago, things in my life have greatly improved. I have made amazing progress in many ways, with a few setbacks along the way.

I lost my job in 2019 because a division of the pharmacy where I worked was purchased by a new pharmacy, which did not hire me. No hard feelings at all. I've managed to survive on adequate unemployment benefits, and, after that, other sources of income.

In September of 2020, I started to have some very strange symptoms which caused much inconvenience and physical distress. Shortly afterwards, after consulting with a neurologist on line (approx. 115 miles away), he diagnosed me with Parkinson's Disease, and prescribed a medication which turned out to be highly helpful, though many "symptoms" remained. In June of 2023 I met with a local neurologist in person, which was one of the best things that ever happened to me. He theorized that a certain medication that I had been taking for over a decade can cause side effects that mimic the symptoms of Parkinson's Disease, and that an accurate diagnosis could be determined only after six months after discontinuing the questionable medication. Fortunately, the proper professional was able to meet with me later that same week, and she authorized me to taper off the medication. My "symptoms" have greatly declined since then, and my levels of motivation and energy have greatly improved.

I have also been involved in local meetings and clubs for mentally ill and other disadvantaged individuals. One meeting that I attended for several months was a "WRAP" meeting (Wellness Recovery Action Plan), and it was highly helpful. It carefully documented the effects of a "trigger." A trigger could be something totally unintended, totally innocent, or even benevolent, that consciously or subconsciously reminded someone of a highly painful event, person, or situation from the very distant past. Earlier in this book I mentioned a girl, Tracy, who was two years behind me in high school, whom I resented as a malicious flirt who tried to set me up for a disappointment. I later realized, 47 years too late, that at first and up to her rejection of me at the dance, I did not regard her as a flirt, and had no reasons to be cynical of her. She indeed, with hardly any exceptions, was friendlier, more cordial, and more enthusiastic toward me than anyone else I ever knew, yet I was highly rude and cynical toward her. I recently realized that this was because Tracy was a trigger, though a totally innocent and benevolent trigger. She subconsciously reminded me of a woman from the distant past who resembled her, who was highly cruel to me. I placed the guilt of this woman whom Tracy resembled onto Tracy, who was totally innocent.

A few weeks later, I suddenly remembered a television advertisement from the mid-1960's for a brand of toilet paper (or "bathroom tissue" as the paper industry desperately wants us to call it). This ad ended with a woman in a soft voice saying, "Touch it." This ending immediately traumatized me. I saw the ad a couple more times, hoping in vain that it would end differently. After that, when the ad appeared on television I would run out of the room, into the bathroom, flush the toilet or turn on the faucet, to drown out the noise of the offensive ending. Well over 55 years later, I theorized that I had been molested, or at least inappropriately touched, during my infancy. That was why I found the ending "Touch it" to be traumatic. Of course, since this touching happened during my infancy, before I was three years of age, it would be impossible to remember it, or to prove that it actually happened.

Then I put two and two together, and concluded that Tracy, who was so innocent and benevolent, physically resembled the woman who molested me, through no fault of her own. To most people, Tracy was highly attractive, and though I barely knew her, was one of the most popular students in her class.

Though I have not seen her in person in over 47 years, except possibly at the local YMCA several months ago, when a woman who looked like her greeted me very enthusiastically, though not by name. I now realize that Tracy was one of the best opportunities that I was ever offered, and that my rude treatment of her was one of my biggest mistakes ever. (I recently tallied my biggest mistakes of my life; my mistreatment of her was number five.) I very deeply regret my rude treatment of her. I have learned that she had a happy marriage, good children, a decent middle-class career, and a fine home. I am glad that she did so well in life.

I have come to appreciate the special things in life and the positive people and events in my life. My grandmother was so precious and lovable and lived until I was 25. I am grateful that my parents lived well into my adult years. They were not perfect, of course, but I owe them very much, especially since I was a special-needs child. Many others have been far less fortunate; my parents both invested their retirement funds wisely so that my brother and I could have a large inheritance.

I am deeply indebted to Danielle, who did so much to improve and enrich my life, who was the best thing that ever happened to me up to that time, who transformed me from a mean hellion into a much more decent person; the staff at Genevaville noticed a big change in me shortly after she arrived. Without her, I would have been stuck at Genevaville for many more months. Before she arrived, nobody was predicting my departure in the near future from Genevaville; soon afterwards, the powers-that-be predicted my near discharge from Genevaville. If she had not met her demise so young, I would owe her the rest of my life to repay her for all that she made possible for me.

Even though a large majority of the residents at Genevaville were two-faced at best, and of frighteningly low character, at least some were a mixed bag, (not consistently bad) and I still get some laughs when thinking of them more than 50 years later. And, before I met Danielle, I was of equally low character as most of them.

I am grateful for my aunt Diana for her relationship with me. She is a very kind, compassionate person.

I am grateful for two very special friends from the 1980's, Fred and Gloria, with whom I have kept in contact all these years.

Our surrounding culture, with its materialistic values, does much to promote ingratitude and envy, as do many politically-motivated agitators. They encourage us to be resentful because most of us are not as wealthy as some; while the Scriptures tell us to be content with a sufficiency (1 Timothy 6:6-10). I have a sufficiency, and am content with such; in doing so I feel that I am practicing equality, even though Politically Correct agitators would argue that as a "white male" I am incapable of practicing equality. I am practicing equality by being content with, and grateful with, a sufficiency; I am doing more to practice equality than anyone of any race, gender, ethnicity, or nationality who is wealthy, insatiably greedy and wants more. When people become greedy, they become oppressors, no matter how "oppressed" they were previously. While I neither support or condone discrimination against anyone by race or gender, greed is evil and oppressive. In addition, greed is idolatry and contrary to the Kingdom of God. (Ephesians 5:5) Greed makes us ungrateful for our possessions and other blessings in life. I have a decent reliable vehicle for transportation; it is sufficient; I need it for transportation; I do not NEED an exclusive vehicle at three times the price in order to impress yuppies.

I am grateful for my Katherine, my girlfriend since 1999. We have had so many special times together. She has powerfully destroyed my feelings of loneliness. Not only that, but she has a very beautiful heart-shaped face! A heart-shaped woman's face is the most beautiful thing in the world!

Instead of comparing ourselves to the small minority that is so wealthy, and resenting how most of us are less privileged than they, we should be comparing ourselves to those less fortunate, who are the large minority of humanity (chiefly in the Third World but many nationally and locally) and working for a sufficiency for all. Losing most of my coin collection was very liberating for me; being a numismaholic caused much greed, ingratitude, selfishness, and insensitivity to the needs of others. I am much happier without it than I ever was with it.

I am grateful for faith in my Lord and Savior Jesus Christ, and pray that every human being will know the love that God has for them in Christ. Those of us who call ourselves Christians have failed miserably to make others aware of this divine love. We variously have mixed our message with exclusive political messages of both the Left and the Right, along with other failures and much toxicity. It is frighteningly exclusive to hear of the Insurrection of January 6, 2021, when protesters held signs and banners of "Jesus Saves," and also when theological progressives mix their theology with Political Correctness. Jesus loves everyone, and the world needs this message. My apologies to the Schaefer Brewing Company, but Jesus is the One Hope to have when you can have only one, and is the Greatest Hope at all other times. God loves every Tom, Dick, Harry, Bob, Carol, Ted, Alice, Wayne, Rebecca, Peter, Natalie, and everyone else.

It is my hope that this autistic autobiography will be a blessing to all. God grant it!